HOMESCHOOL PSYCH:

Preparing Christian Homeschool Students for Psychology 101

Tim Rice, D. Min.

Homeschool Psych:
Preparing Christian Homeschool Students for Psychology 101

Internet: www.homeschoolpsych.com

Cover Design: Tina and Abigail Rice and Kyle Caldwell
Marketing Manager: Kyle Caldwell
Illustrations: Melissa Rice
Research Assistant: Daniel Rice
Field Testing: Katie Rice

Table of Contents

A Christian Worldview, Psychology, and Homeschooling?

Psychology is one of the most controversial and divisive academic subjects among Christians today. If you have never considered introductory psychology, your Christian worldview, and homeschooling in the same thought, do it now. Ask yourself if psychology has a place alongside biology, chemistry, and physics in your homeschool and consider how psychology fits (if it fits at all) with your Christian worldview. Some Christians accept psychology wholesale, some reject it entirely, and some wrestle with which aspects to accept and which to reject. Some Christians view psychology as an important academic discipline, consistent with a Christian worldview, and worthy of study. Others view psychology as an idolatrous and ungodly rival religion. Some describe it as "psychobabble," "psycho-heresy," and the most deadly form of modernism to ever confront the Church (Bobgan and Bobgan, 1987). Whatever you believe about psychology, the time to address academic psychology is BEFORE leaving home to go to college.

If you go to college, there is an excellent chance you will take an introductory (at least) psychology course. Christian students are often ill-prepared to confront the criticisms of Christianity and the anti-Christian worldview presented by modern psychology. The material taught in introductory psychology courses WILL challenge your worldview. University level instruction in modern psychology is generally atheistic and humanistic. Psychology departments often are home to the most anti-Christian intellectuals on college campuses. As a group, psychology professors have high levels of agnosticism, skepticism, and atheism (Jones, as cited in Grace & Ecklund, 1995). The psychology professor is unlikely to be sympathetic to your Christian worldview and may attack your faith as unscientific, irrational, prudish, exploitive, controlling, inhibitive, oppressive, and naïve. Many in psychology suggest that Christianity is incompatible with sound mental health and that the Christian faith contributes more to human suffering than to its alleviation (Watters, 1987).

You are probably well prepared to defend your faith and well prepared to directly refute humanism, evolutionism, empiricism, determinism, relativism, reductionism, and naturalism (the core philosophical assumptions of modern psychology). In introductory psychology classes, those core worldview assumptions are presented under the banner of "science and are often subtle and difficult to recognize. Failure to recognize anti-Christian assumptions embodied in psychological theories may lead Christian students to accept ideas that are inconsistent with a Christian worldview. Psychology courses, even in Christian colleges and universities, rarely distinguish philosophical assumptions from science. C. S. Lewis once observed that Christian faith is not very likely to be shaken by a book on an alternate worldview (Lewis, 1952). However, if that worldview were embedded in books on Biology, Politics, Astronomy, or Psychology, that might shake us.

Secular humanistic philosophies, common in colleges and universities, influence Christian students and many Christians walk away from their faith during college (LifeWay Research, 2007). Christian students in higher education face direct challenges from straightforward anti-Christian teaching and subtle challenges from anti-Christian assumptions integrated into otherwise benign material. The subtle danger remains strong if homeschoolers fail to address an entire academic discipline (psychology) by wrongly equating the discipline with its modern underlying assumptions. The goal of Christian education, in biology, history, theology, the arts, and in psychology, is to understand God's creation and, in the words of Johannes Kepler, to "think God's thoughts after him." As Christians assert a Christian worldview in the university, asserting that worldview in psychology is appropriate and timely. Christians have a duty to reclaim the whole culture and Christian homeschoolers have an opportunity to lead that effort. The involvement of homeschoolers in the study of psychology is an integral part of that effort.

This text was developed for Christian homeschoolers as a prerequisite to college–level introductory psychology and is intended to help prepare student to think "Christianly" about psychology's concepts, and more importantly, its underlying worldview assumptions. This text examines the Christian criticisms of psychology and explains the pitfalls students face in university study of psychology but does not accept that those pitfalls are justification for rejecting the entire academic discipline. Instead, this text suggests that the study of the soul, the mind, and behavior are right and proper for Christians and that Christian students should join the contemporary psychological conversation and become part of the future intellectual leadership in psychology.

Section I is intended to help prepare Christian homeschoolers for the worldview challenges of modern psychology. Section II is an overview of key concepts commonly taught in introductory psychology and provides opportunities with which you can study psychology more deeply. The author suggests that you create a notebook in which you complete the assignments and the opportunities for further study. The assignments were created to encourage you to begin thinking "Christianly" about psychology. If you discover a broken web link, visit www.homeschoolpsych.com or email tim@homeschoolpsych.com for alternate links.

"What is man? To this question psychology seeks an answer."
E. G. Boring 1939

"What is man, that thou art mindful of him?" Psalms 8:4

Psychology is much more than Freud, Prozac, and Ritalin.
Tim Rice

Read Matthew 22:37. What does it mean to love the Lord your God with all your heart? What does it mean to love the Lord with all your mind? What is the nature of your "heart?" What is the nature of your "mind?" Does loving the Lord with our mind include a *duty* to humbly investigate God's creation? Does the duty to humbly investigate God's creation extend to His grandest creation: Mankind? Does that duty extend to Mankind's mind? If so, one could argue that Christians have a *duty* to study psychology. If Christ is Lord of all, He is Lord of theology, education, biology, homeschooling, and psychology.

This chapter defines psychology and describes its extent in modern society, academia, and the Church. Chapter 2 explores the nature of a Christian worldview and Chapters 3 – 6 examine the worldview assumptions common in modern psychology and contrasts those assumptions with a Christian worldview, with the goal of helping you to wrestle with the relationship of your worldview to modern psychology.

What is Psychology?

What do you think when you meet a psychologist, counselor, or a student majoring in psychology? Many think that studying psychology means learning to analyze, manipulate, or control people. Some think psychology is about powerful psychiatric drugs or reclining on a therapist's couch to talk about why you hate your mother.

Psychology is much more. The American Psychological Association recognizes over 50 psychology divisions. Psychologists study the brain, the relationship between the brain and behavior, and the relationship between the environment and behavior. Psychology is about how we process information, what motivates us, how we remember, and how we learn, feel, and perceive. Preparation for a study of psychology requires the Christian student to understand the foundations of a Christian worldview and the foundations of modern psychology.

> **Assignment 1.1**
>
> **Define:**
> **Assumption**
> **Benign**
> **Contemporary**
> **Continuum**
> **Divisive**
> **Heresy**
> **Inherent**
> **Modernism**
> **Philosophy**
> **Prerequisite**
> **Secular Humanism**
> **Sine qua non**
> **Usurpation**

Assignment 1.2

Visit http://www.apa.org/about/division.html. Review the Divisions of the American Psychological Association and visit the homepage for a few of the divisions to explore the extent of psychological topics.

The word psychology has meaning in much the same way as the words religion, philosophy, and politics. Those words have different (and sometimes contradictory) meanings to different people. For some, "psychology" is synonymous with "psychotherapy." For others psychology means a type of mind control and manipulation. The American Heritage Dictionary defines psychology as "the science that deals with mental processes and behavior" and "the branch of philosophy that studies the soul, the mind, and the relationship of life and mind to the functions of the body."

"Mental processes" refers to human emotions, memories, thoughts, drives, perceptions, development, learning, personality, and relationships. "Psychology" shares the same etymology as the words "spirit" and "soul" leading some to conclude that psychology, in its original meaning, referred to spiritual content. A full understanding of the word psychology includes the study of how Mankind is like other creatures and the study of how Mankind is uniquely created in the image of God. By examining God's natural revelation, guided by special revelation, psychology should seek understanding of how we are like the animals and how we are unique in our God-likeness.

Assignment 1.3

Define:
Etymology

Assignment: 1.4

Visit http://www.geocities.com/etalk99/strongs.html. Enter Strong's # 5590 for NT references for psuche {psoo-khay}. Review Biblical usage of psuche, read verses containing the word psuche, and compare and contrast meanings of psuche with modern definitions of psychology.

Over time psychology has been described as:

Assignment 1.5

Define:
Amelioration
Pathology

1. The scientific study of human life and human nature.
2. The science of mental life.
3. That division of science that takes human behavior as its subject.
4. Attempts to identify, describe, and classify the general laws of the behavior of living organisms.
5. The scientific study of the soul/behavior/mind.
6. The scientific study of how living creatures interact with their environment and each other.
7. A body of thought for understanding, measuring, assessing, and possibly changing people's emotions, thoughts, perceptions, and behaviors.
8. The emotional and behavioral characteristics of an individual or group.
9. Actions or arguments used to manipulate or influence others.
10. A branch of philosophy that studies the soul, the mind, and the relationship of the soul and mind to the functions of the body.
11. A system for describing human personality.
12. A system for describing emotional and behavioral pathology and strategies for their amelioration.

> **Psychiatry is the branch of medicine that deals with the diagnosis, treatment, and prevention of mental and emotional disorders.**

The Extent of Psychology

For its young age, modern psychology has had remarkable impact. Psychology is popular and deeply imbedded in society, academia, and the Church. Modern society is fascinated with all things psychological. Each year Americans buy millions of books on self-help, addiction, recovery, relationships, parenting, spiritual growth, and emotional and mental health. Most Americans will seek mental health services or be exposed to psychological practices at some point. Psychology influences business, advertising, social work, nursing, engineering, and the Church.

Nowhere is the extent of psychology's influence more evident than in academia. Most medical schools, liberal arts colleges, seminaries, and teachers colleges require students to have some exposure to psychology, and psychology is one of the most popular undergraduate majors at public and Christian colleges and universities (Astin, 1993). College enrollment in psychology courses outpaces every other scientific discipline. Many high schools now offer an introductory psychology course.

Assignment 1.6

Define:
Agnosticism
Atheism
Determinism
Empiricism
Evolutionism
Humanism
Naturalism
Reductionism
Relativism

The extent of psychology is not limited to the culture and academia. The Christian church's fascination with psychology closely mirrors the world's. Psychology is widespread in the church and Christians flock to psychology. Churches, Bible colleges, seminaries, and Christian radio promote psychological programs. Christian colleges and universities offer introductory psychology classes and degree programs and many have established psychology doctoral programs. Christian colleges and universities offer courses in Christian Marriage, Ethics in Psychology, Integration of Psychology and Christianity, and Biblical Psychology. Psychological insights influence sermons across the country and some pastors leave the pulpit for pastoral counseling or social work. Self-help, recovery, addiction, relationships, and personal, emotional, or mental health make up the bulk of the new Christian book titles.

A Christian Approach to Psychology

The first essential attitude for the Christian studying psychology is respect for the complete inspiration and authority of the Scriptures. We must maintain a commitment to the authority and inspiration of Scripture and not underestimate the corrupting, distorting, and destructive influence of sin on human thinking. We need to remember that all truth is God's Truth and that ultimately there will be no conflict between true psychology and a Christian worldview. Christians studying and working in psychology must be faithful to Scripture, not compromise their Christian worldview assumptions, and must understand modern psychology's historical roots, philosophical assumptions, and empirical methods.

Our study of psychology must be more than a curiosity to discover something interesting about people. A Christian approach to the study of psychology should be evangelic. Christians studying and working in psychology must increase and effectively communicate the body of evidence supporting the Christian worldview as the most logical, internally consistent, and meaningful. We must see a spiritual purpose to our study. When a non-Christian recognizes that he has accepted as truth (by faith) psychology's philosophical assumptions, he may be closer to accepting God's Truth (by a saving faith). Christians studying psychology have, among their classmates and professors, a ripe mission field.

We should answer those who attack Christianity on psychological grounds with a sound apologia. We must provide a solid defense for our own assumptions. The Christian studying psychology should be humble. We cannot arrogantly claim that we have all the answers or that we can "prove" our positions. We must be willing to hold contradictory beliefs until better data or clearer revelation reveals there is no genuine contradiction.

We must remember that all learning is, at least in part, the work of the Holy Spirit and that only the Holy Spirit can reveal God's ultimate Truth. As the Holy Spirit guides us, we become more Christ-like, which in turn, affects our scholarship. We must resist theological hubris by claiming that our theological beliefs are superior to, or automatically "truer" than psychological findings. To do so makes a mockery of the unifying nature of God's full revelation. Conversely, Christians in psychology should confront other Christians who "popularize" or "Christianize" heretical beliefs by sprinkling in a few verses of the New Testament and mentioning Jesus.

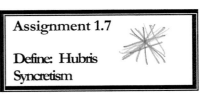

Assignment 1.7

Define: Hubris
Syncretism

Christians studying and working in psychology can help reduce the Church's misunderstanding and fear of psychology and help remove the stigma of seeking help for emotional problems. We must help the Church fulfill its duty to minister to the world's psychological needs. Christians studying psychology must have excellent preparation in theology, biblical interpretation, and the principles of Christian discipleship. Do not study psychology without the full armor of God. You must understand the rich history of Christian psychology stretching from the early Church. Though most Christians who study psychology understand that the Bible ought to influence their scholarship, too many Christians in psychology know far more about psychology than they do about their own religious traditions.

Christians in psychology must prevent modern psychology from corrupting their view of the nature of God, Mankind, knowledge, right and wrong, and psychopathology while effectively and lovingly correcting those already corrupted. We must wrestle with freedom vs. determinism vs. responsibility vs. heredity vs. environment and the concept of the self. We must produce rigorous scholarship and research to develop a body of authentically Christian psychological data (Collins, 2000). We need not bracket our faith in order to practice science and we need not defend Christ from research. We can then apply our insight to topics dear to Christian ministry. For example:

- What variables account for the failures and successes of Christian ministries?
- What factors contribute to the large percentage of dropouts among second generation Christians?

- Can research support the beneficial effects of prayer and medication?
- Can research into the nature and causes of anger help fathers avoid provoking their children to anger?
- Why do some who use pornography become pedophiles and others not?
- Can psychology devise tests for assessing spiritual maturity for leadership positions in the church?
- Can psychology devise tests to help determine if missionaries are prepared for the struggles of foreign missions?
- What is the optimal size of small group Bible studies?
- What is the most effective treatment for cultic brainwashing?
- What is the relationship of the spiritual disciplines to physical health?
- What styles of parenting are most likely to produce Christian character traits in children?
- Has educational psychology made discoveries beneficial to homeschoolers?
- How can we improve training for Christian workers?
- Can Christians in psychology contribute to our understanding of interpersonal violence, holocausts and genocide, deception, retardation, schizophrenia, psychosis, developmental disorders, post-traumatic stress disorder, divorce, homicide, suicide, gender roles, euthanasia, abortion, grief, prejudice, and the psychological effects of disability and chronic illness?

In addition to exemplary scholarship, Christians studying and working in psychology must live exemplary lives (Myers, 1996). We must, like Christ, live the true psychology. We must reclaim psychology for Christ. Chuck Colson suggests that there is a "cultural commission," similar to the Great Commission that requires Christians (including Christian homeschoolers), to "reclaim" the culture, education, and by extension, psychology. The Church risks marginalization if Christians ignore their responsibility to reclaim the whole culture (including academic psychology). The early Church showed God's way to be so much better that even the pagans recognized it. Should we do any less with psychology? Christians who study psychology join others in physics, biology, history, the arts, sociology, and many other fields seeking a deeper understanding of all of God's creation.

Each of us has foundational beliefs about the world. Our view of the world is influenced by those beliefs.

Chapter 2

This chapter defines worldview and describes those components of a worldview in which modern psychology and Christianity conflict. The Apostle Paul warned the Church at Corinth to resist unbelief and to submit every thought to the obedience of Christ. At a minimum, Paul's instructions require Christians to examine the theories, interpretations, and worldview assumptions of modern psychology through the lens of a Christian worldview. Each of us has a set of lenses or core foundational beliefs through which we view the world. Those lenses and beliefs define our Christian worldview. You must be grounded in a Christian worldview and be able to identify the worldview assumptions woven throughout psychological theories.

> The metaphor of a worldview as a set of lenses is insufficient to fully describe how Christians should interact with psychology. Lenses and filters are passive. Christians should proactively think "Christianly" about psychology. Many suggest that Christians today have lost the ability to think Christianly.

What are the components of a Christian Worldview?

Though some suggest there are as many as ten foundational beliefs in a Christian worldview. Psychology and a Christian worldview intersect around five major issues:

1. What do you believe about God?
2. What do you believe about the nature of Mankind?
3. What do you believe about the nature of knowledge?
4. What do you believe about the nature of right and wrong?
5. What do you believe about the causes of and cures for mental suffering?

God exists or He does not. Your view of God includes whether you believe He exists, what you believe about God (His character), and the extent to which He influences your life. A Christian worldview holds that there is one true God who is personal, loving, just, infinite, self-revealing, all-powerful, all knowing, ever present, self-existent, sovereign, and eternal.

Your view of Mankind includes whether you believe that we are inherently "good" or not and whether you believe that we are the purposeful creation of God or the product of purposeless forces. A Christian worldview sees Mankind as created in the likeness and image of God and as sinners in rebellion against God by nature and by choice. One's view of Mankind also includes whether or not we each have an eternal spirit, soul, and/or mind that exists independent of our physical bodies.

Your view of the nature of right and wrong includes whether you believe that there are absolute rules governing human behavior and whether there are consequences for violating those rules. A Christian worldview recognizes moral absolutes described in Scripture and lived by Jesus Christ.

Your view of the nature of knowledge includes whether you believe science is the only valid path to knowledge. Is the scientific method the only way we can "know" anything? Is the Bible the only valid source of knowledge about the nature of Mankind? A Christian worldview holds that God reveals Himself in His creation (nature), Scripture, and supremely in His Son. This worldview sees the universe operating in accordance with orderly natural laws but allows for supernatural intervention.

Your view of the causes of and cures for mental suffering includes whether you believe that pain, suffering, and guilt have meaning and purpose or are unfortunate circumstances to be avoided at all costs. A Christian worldview holds that through pain we are refined and made more Christ-like. The Christian worldview believes that redemption and restoration makes us "whole" but that "wholeness" does not necessarily equal ease and comfort. Christians disagree about whether extra-biblical techniques are proper approaches to caring for mental suffering.

ALL psychological theories are constructed

> **Assignment 2.1**
>
> **Define:**
> **Amelioration**
> **Empirical**
> **Omnipotent**
> **Omnipresent**
> **Omniscient**
> **Pathology**
> **Remediation**
>
> **Describe how the ancient heresies of Gnosticism and Pelagianism fit with your Christian worldview.**
>
> **Define, compare, and contrast empiricism and Gnosticism.**

> **Assignment 2.2**
> **Define:**
>
> **Paradigm**
> **Teleology**

around a worldview. One's worldview explicitly or implicitly guides the development of theories and even influences the designs and outcomes of experiments. It is important to understand that everyone's worldview is a matter of faith. No one's worldview is a matter of science. The point is crucial. The foundational beliefs of a Christian worldview, of an atheist's worldview, and of a psychology professor's worldview are matters of faith and philosophy and not of data and science. The conflicts between modern psychology's worldview and a Christian worldview are common to all sciences; not just psychology. In fact, the conflicts between psychology and a Christian worldview are just one manifestation of historical conflicts between "faith" and "science."

The Development of Modern Psychology: View of God - Theism or Naturalism?

The establishment of modern scientific psychology, independent from philosophy and religion, dates to 1879 and the founding of Wilhelm Wundt's psychological laboratory in Germany. As modern psychology developed, it emphasized that psychology was a natural science. The application of natural science methods to the study of psychology was new and heralded psychology's entry into the realm or natural sciences. It is not

> Naturalism in psychology is the belief that there is no God and that natural causes alone are sufficient to explain everything that exists. In psychology, naturalism is a belief that all behavior and mental processes, without exception, are a result of the operation of natural forces.

possible to overstate the importance of psychology's claim to be a natural science and of the influence of evolution and atheism on its relationship to a Christian worldview. Psychology's claim to be a natural science profoundly changed its relationship to a Christian worldview.

Every worldview starts with a theory of how the universe began. Naturalism begins with the assumption that forces of nature alone are adequate to explain everything that exists. In terms of psychology, one's position on whether Mankind is the creation of a personal and supernatural God or the product of a natural process could not be more crucial. As a Christian student, you must approach every discipline, including psychology, from the vantage point of faith, refusing to replace your theistic assumptions with naturalism.

The movement toward the natural sciences even contributed to psychology's definition evolving from "the study of the mind, spirit, or soul" to "the science of the brain and behavior." Psychology distanced itself from its philosophical-religious traditions. Psychology relegated religion to that part of human experience dealing with mysticism and rituals. Psychology came to be seen by many as part of a scientific replacement for the pronouncements of the Bible.

Since Wundt, modern psychology has refined the uses of experimental methods to study Mankind. However, a myopic focus on natural processes and the scientific method causes modern psychology to fall short in its ability to explore the fullness of Mankind and leaves teleological questions unanswerable.

Assignment 2.1

Based on your knowledge of Charles Darwin's Origin of Species and its implications on modern biology, write an essay in which you discuss how evolutionary thought might influence psychology.

It is noteworthy that psychology's paradigm shift was part of a bigger intellectual-cultural movement in the late 19th century. Naturalistic, evolutionary, and atheistic assumptions led to the "modernization" of a number of sciences (most notably Biology). Many of the "fathers" of modern psychology took their training with Wundt and that first generation of modern psychologists worked to distinguish psychology from philosophy and religion. Today modern psychology remains predominately naturalistic. The application of naturalism to a topic so dear to Christians (What is the nature of Mankind?) is largely responsible to the vitriolic condemnations of the entire academic discipline.

Flowing logically from naturalistic assumptions, early psychologists described Mankind as "machines," "things," and "objects of study." As modern psychology integrated Darwin's theory of evolution, modern psychology moved further from its Biblical and historical view of Mankind.

For further study: Using reference material from *Studies in the History of Science and Christianity* at http://www.asa3.org/ASA/topics/history/index.html.

Write an essay describing how Biblical theism provides the foundation of science.

Using reference material of your choice, write a second essay to respond to this statement; "Christians should reject any use of natural science methods to understand Mankind." Your response must consider Romans 1:25.

The Development of Modern Psychology: View of God - Darwinian Evolution

Understanding the influence of Darwinian evolution on psychology and on **EVERY** academic discipline is crucial.

C. S. Lewis once observed that:	Consider this modification of Lewis' quote:
"Our faith is not very likely to be shaken by any book on Hinduism. But if, whenever we read an elementary book on Geology, Botany, Politics, or Astronomy, we found that its implications were Hindu, that would shake us. It is not the books written in direct defense of materialism that make the modern man a materialist; it is the materialistic assumptions in all the other books."	Our faith is not very likely to be shaken by any book on Evolution. But if, whenever we read an elementary book on Psychology, we found that its implications were evolutionary, that would shake us. It is not the books written in direct defense of evolution that make the modern man an evolutionist; it is the evolutionary assumptions in all the other books.

Assignment 2.2
Do a web search of the following phrases:
Social Darwinism, Economic Darwinism, Political Darwinism, Legal Darwinism, Educational Darwinism. Based on your observations of the application of Darwinian evolution to sociology, economics, politics, the law, and education, write an essay describing how Darwinian evolution might influence psychology.

As in Geology, Botany, and Politics, Christian students must be able to recognize evolutionary assumptions embedded in psychological theories.

Herbert Spencer, a contemporary of Charles Darwin, extended evolution into psychology. Evolutionists since Spencer have sought evolutionary explanations for the complexity of the human mind under the assumption that innate principles operating in living organisms propel them to proceed upward in complexity. Applied to psychology, evolution explains the human mind and all mental functioning in terms of beneficial traits passed genetically from one generation to the next. Mental disorders become vestiges of behavior left over from earlier stages of evolution. Morality is simply beneficial tendencies chosen by natural selection. Freud applied evolution to describe Mankind's behavior in terms of a primitive (most animal-like) "id" and a more evolved "ego." Everything about

Mankind, from marital relationships to love, hate, guilt, remorse, gratitude, envy, kindness, faithfulness, friendships, sibling relationships, self-control, and even office politics have been "explained" in terms of the evolutionary forces.

The evolutionary influences in modern psychology are inconsistent with a Christian worldview and not essential to a study of psychology. Darwinian evolution imposed itself on the Christian understanding of psychology and then tried to exclude anything Christian (Reber, 2006). Though evolutionary thinkers assert evolution as fact, it is nonetheless a worldview assumption ultimately grounded in faith. The evolution debate, in psychology as in all science, is not a matter of religion against science; it is a matter of one faith against another (Ham, 1987).

You are studying what?

Assignment 2.3

For many Christian families, countering evolutionary teaching was a factor in the decision to homeschool. Those evolutionary assumptions, expressed in modern psychology, have led many of Christians to reject the discipline completely. There is not, however a similar call for Christians to reject biology (the academic discipline most influenced by evolutionary thought).

Write an essay suggesting explanations why, using curricula written from a Christian perspective, Christian homeschoolers confront evolutionary assumptions in modern biology but have not taken a similar approach to psychology.

The Bottom Line

The bottom line is that, beginning with Darwin's *Origin of Species*, all sciences, including psychology, underwent a transformation. Scientific data was interpreted in ways to exclude supernatural beliefs and assumptions. Psychology, once the study of the soul, became the study of the brain and behavior. Darwinian evolution imposed itself on the Christian understanding of life (biology) and then excluded the possibility of the supernatural. Likewise, Darwinian evolution imposed itself on the Christian understanding of Mankind (psychology) and then tried to exclude anything Christian.

The Development of Modern Psychology: View of God - Atheism

Recall that one's worldview includes what one believes about God. The Christian view recognizes the existence of God as Creator and Sustainer of everything and Author of all Truth. Many of the "fathers" of modern psychology however, were more than indifferent to a Christian worldview; they opposed it. Sigmund Freud predicted that science would replace religion. He viewed organized religion as a "universal obsessional neurosis, infantile helplessness," and "regression to primary narcissistic expression of neurotic tendencies." G. Stanley Hall, William James, John Dewey, J. B. Watson, B. F. Skinner, Carl Jung, Karen Horney, Erich Fromm, Jean Piaget, Carl Rogers and Abraham Maslow saw their work as offering sound alternatives to Christian explanations of man. They and many others strongly rejected Biblical knowledge and contended that modern science made Christianity permanently out of date.

Chapter

3

Then God said, "Let Us make man in Our image, according to Our likeness."

Mankind has debated the essence of human nature for centuries. In psychology, the nature of Mankind is fundamental to all theoretical formulations. A Christian worldview includes a Biblical description of the essence of human nature (**Biblical anthropology**). Modern psychology does not. Biblical anthropology best describes the complexity of human nature, but it does not answer every question about our brains and behavior. Biblical anthropology may not answer every question about our brains and behavior, but is does provide a complete and sufficient foundation for living. You do not need to reject a Biblical anthropology to study psychology. This chapter begins with the foundation of Biblical anthropology and moves to a review of the assumptions about Mankind characteristic of modern psychology's major theories.

The Development of Modern Psychology: View of Mankind

Every psychological "model" of Mankind is grounded in assumptions. Assumptions, by definition, are not facts. They are held by faith. Each of the "grand psychological theories" is distinguishable from others by its assumptions. Every personality theory makes implicit or explicit assumptions about the nature of Mankind. Research data is interpreted in terms of those assumptions.

Biblical anthropology is that part of theology dealing

Structuralism describes mental experiences as complex structures comprised of from simpler component structures. Early psychologists sought to discover the "structure" of mental processes and the laws governing their formation.

Functionalism focused not on the structure of consciousness but on its purpose or function.

Freudian psychology focused on the nature of unconscious mental processes.

Behaviorists emphasized behavior over conscious and unconscious mental processes.

with the nature of Mankind. The foundation of Biblical anthropology and, by extension, the foundation of a Christian approach to the study of psychology is that, on the one hand, Mankind was created by a loving God in His image. On the other hand, Mankind was made from the dust of the earth and is part of the "natural" order. We are both God-like and animal-like. Physically, we are like the animals. We are born, we grow old, and our bodies eventually die. However, like God, we are spiritual beings. As such, a comprehensive psychological description of the nature of Mankind must recognize our God-likeness. Though created in the image of God, the fall changed us. We are all sinners by birth and by choice; restored and renewed in salvation and sanctification. Unlike the animals, we have moral discernment, freedom to choose, and responsibility for our behavior. We are relational beings. We are more than products of conditioning, unmet needs, chemical imbalances, and traumas. We are not autonomous, we are more than the sum of our parts, and more than complex machines in closed cause-and-effect systems.

The Development of Modern Psychology: View of Mankind – Sigmund Freud

Sigmund Freud was a tremendously important figure in the development of modern psychology's view of Mankind. His theories of personality and psychoanalysis continue to influence thinkers in many disciplines and thoroughly permeate academia and the culture. No class in business, economics, education, sociology, philosophy, and of course psychology, is complete until Freud's influence is considered.

Freudian psychoanalysis is based on a belief that we are often not consciously aware of factors that influence our emotions and behavior. Freud anticipated that his approach to counseling would someday replace pastoral care. Freud's view of Mankind focused on the unconscious and he believed that the conscious aspects of personality are secondary to the mysterious and hidden subconscious. The conflict between the conscious and unconscious mind (not sin and responsibility) is the hallmark of a Freudian view of Mankind. Freud described levels of consciousness (conscious, pre-conscious, and unconscious), the components of personality (Id, Ego, and Superego), and the mechanisms by which the unconscious influences our personality. According to Freud, unconscious sexual drives (the libido) are key to the maturation through the stages of personality development (oral, anal, phallic, latency and genital stages). Many of Freud's defense mechanisms (strategies to protect the ego from anxiety) are part of our common vocabulary.

Freud was a major figure in the development of modern psychiatry and counseling. A Christian response to Freudian psychology begins at the worldview level. Freud's worldview was not consistent with Scripture. Freud was an atheist who in later writings made clear his belief that God did not exist. To Freud, God was an ego defense mechanism born of id anxiety. His theories represent an atheistic worldview. Because Freud attempted to define the human condition without reference to God, a Christian studying psychology is wise to view all his theories with great skepticism.

Assignment 3.1

Review a biography of Sigmund Freud and summary of this theories at:
http://fates.cns.muskingum.edu/~psych/psycweb/history/freud.htm

Read an article on the influence of Freud at:
http://www.time.com/time/time100/scientist/profile/freud.html

---

The Development of Modern Psychology: View of Mankind - Behaviorism

Behaviorism, a movement in early modern psychology, described Mankind as very complicated machines that react to stimuli in predictable ways. Early modern psychologists emphasized measurable and observable behavior, avoided the study of intangible mental processes, and avoided questions of meaning and purpose (teleology) in the name of science and to distinguish the discipline from philosophy. Strict behaviorists believed that they would eventually explain all human behavior in terms of learned responses to environmental stimuli. B. F. Skinner, a "radical behaviorist" proposed that ALL human behavior was determined by the environment and not free. He believed that humans do not have even a limited ability to transcend environmental influences and that we operate as closed cause-and-effect systems. Skinner believed freedom and responsibility were illusions.

Scripture does not support the ideas of strict behaviorism or rigid determinism. A Christian worldview balances God's sovereignty with human freedom and responsibility. A Christian worldview does not exclude an element of predictability in human behavior and provides many examples of God's use of rewards and consequences. A Christian worldview recognizes that rewards and consequences are important to learning but does not view Mankind as robots, programmed by environmental stimuli or childhood experiences. We have minds, will, foresight, judgment, and the ability and responsibility to control our impulses. It is essential that Christians studying psychology grapple with the theological issues of determinism, free-will, choice, and responsibility. Any acceptable Christian view of psychology must be consistent with a Biblical view of determinism and responsibility while acknowledging the lawfulness and predictability of behavior.

For further study:
1. Read Ivan Pavlov biography at:

http://nobelprize.org/nobel_prizes/medicine/laureates/1904/pavlov-bio.html

2. Read Ivan Pavlov's lecture in which he describes his work dogs entitled "Conditioned Reflexes: An Investigation of the Physiological Activity of the Cerebral Cortex" at http://psychclassics.yorku.ca/Pavlov/lecture2.htm.

3. Read Studying the Mind of Animals by John B. Watson at: http://psychclassics.yorku.ca/Watson/Animals/index.htm

---

The Development of Modern Psychology: View of Mankind - Reductionism

If, as strict behaviorists suggest, Mankind is nothing more than complex machines, it follows that the complexity is reducible to simpler underlying parts. The philosophy that complex phenomenon are composed of ever-increasingly simple underlying components is called reductionism. Reductionist psychology was a natural result of efforts to describe Mankind (without reference to God) in solely natural terms. Strict reductionism assumes that all psychological processes, including concepts like love, hope, thought, altruism, and religious experience, can be divided into smaller, analyzable parts. Reductionism underlies modern psychiatry's efforts to "fix" the brain with medications.

Assignment 3.2
Read *Reductionism in the Psychology of the Eighties: Can Biochemistry Eliminate Addiction, Mental Illness, and Pain?* by Stanton Peele at:

http://www.peele.net/lib/reduct.html

The Development of Modern Psychology: View of Mankind - Humanism

Humanism is a philosophy that centers on values, capacities, and worth. Humanism differs from Freudian and behavioral psychology in its emphasis on the emotional, motivational, and social aspects of Mankind. Secular or modern humanism is a philosophy that advocates human rather than religious values, rejects all supernaturalism, and relies solely on reason and science. Secular humanism presumes that God does not exist and that Mankind is the self-existent culmination of evolutionary development. Humanist psychology claims that people can reach full potential in accepting nonjudgmental environments and that in our "natural state," human nature is good. If Mankind is inherently good, then we have within us the potential for self-actualization and there is no need for the Biblical messages of justification and sanctification.

> Pelagianism is a theological doctrine proposed by Pelagius, a British monk, and condemned as heresy by the Roman Catholic Church in A.D. 416. It denied original sin and affirmed the ability of humans to be righteous by the exercise of free will.

> Assignment 3.3
>
> Write an essay to compare and contrast Humanism with Pelagianism then contrast each with the Biblical concepts of justification and sanctification.

The humanist philosophy and Christian worldview differ in their respective understandings of human nature and Mankind's origins. A Christian worldview sees Jesus Christ as the measure of Mankind's "actualization." A secular humanistic approach to Mankind denies the value of self-denial and guilt where a Christian view holds that Mankind paradoxically achieves self-fulfillment through self-renunciation.

For further study:

Read the affirmations of the Humanist Manifesto I, II, and III at www.jcn.com/manifestos.html

Read an Atheist Manifesto at www.truthdig.com/dig/item/200512_an_atheist_manifesto/

Describe in your own words how the philosophies expressed in the readings might influence one's understanding of the nature of the human mind.

The Development of Modern Psychology: View of Mankind - Selfism

Humanistic psychology contributed to a common psychological perspective that people should feel good about themselves, learn to love themselves, and rid themselves of shame and guilt. That perspective is known as "self psychology" or "selfism." Selfism is a philosophy based on a worldview in which personal fulfillment, self-expression, self-acceptance, and self-fulfillment are key to good mental health. A selfist view of man is one in which personal subjective well-being and social functioning is of primary importance and suffering is an absurd man-made mistake.

Selfism is widely popular and the most common position of mental health workers who see "self-esteem" as the foundation of sound mental health. Self-esteem, self-fulfillment, self-expression, self-love, and individualism are appealing ideas. Modern psychology's emphasis on self-esteem is the one assumption of modern psychology that is responsible for the most vitriolic condemnations of psychology from Christians. Unlike other worldviews assumptions of modern psychology, the belief that "good" self-esteem is important has wide acceptance in much of Christendom. Dr. James Dobson speaks of "self-esteem" in terms of God's sacrificial love for His creation. With some Christians viewing self-love as a type of idolatry and others integrating self-esteem into their theology, internecine battles among Christians are not uncommon.

> **Assignment 3:4**
>
> Define:
> Internecine

Mankind is sinful and in revolt against God through the assertion of the self. It is Jesus' example (not a subjective view of happiness) that defines actualization and to which we should strive. Jesus lived the true psychology. Contrition, self-denial, and humility are means by which we achieve spiritual growth. A Christian studying psychology must reconcile those ideas with a recognition that, though pride is a form of idolatry, beings created in God's image do not exalt God by denigrating His creation. The Christian worldview sees self-actualization as glorifying God through obedient service.

The structuralist, functionalist, Freudian, behaviorist, humanistic, and selfist (and others not addressed in this text) descriptions of the nature of Mankind are philosophical positions. Remember that modern psychology sought to distance itself from philosophy and establish itself as a "hard" science. Modern psychology has a tendency to represent itself as a science while proclaiming philosophical theories. Data collected through scientific methods are raw and sterile. Interpretations of data and grand theories (psychologies) built around the data are inherently philosophical. By claiming the mantle of science, psychological theorists assert a false claim of scientific neutrality in their philosophizing. Untenable philosophical belief systems falsely benefit from the respect due to science.

Chapter

4

"I am God, and there is none like me." "As the heavens are higher than the earth, so are my ways higher than your ways and my thoughts than your thoughts" - God

God created psychology when he created man in his own image (Fleck and Carter, 1981).

This text asserted earlier that introductory psychology courses would challenge your Christian worldview. A major component of the challenge (or ridicule) will be epistemological in nature. Psychology professors may assert their worldview assumptions as settled science and ridicule yours as naïve and immature. Unfortunately, your Christian brothers and sisters may challenge your study of psychology as evidence of your spiritual immaturity while asserting that their particular Biblical exegesis is a God-ordained indisputable truth for the ages.

> **Assignment 4.1**
>
> **Define:**
> **Bias**
> **Dichotomy**
> **Epistemology**
> **Objective**
> **Postmodernism**
> **Subjective**

This chapter compares and contrasts the epistemology underlying modern psychology's worldview with that of a Christian worldview. This chapter also examines the epistemological differences that contribute to disagreement among Christians about the study of psychology.

The Development of Modern Psychology: View of Knowledge

How do we know anything with certainty? Epistemology is a core area of philosophy, concerning the nature, sources, and limits of knowledge. A fundamental assumption common to psychological research and a Christian worldview is that truth, objective and independent truth absolutely exists. The process of knowing truth, however, is absolutely subjective.

> **Assignment 4.2**
>
> **Angelology**
> **Anthropology**
> **Bibliology**
> **Christology**
> **Ecclesiology**
> **Eschatology**
> **Hamartiology**
> **Pneumatology**
> **Soteriology**
> **Theology Proper**

A Christian worldview holds that the goal of all knowledge is to understand God's ways. The goal of psychology is knowledge about the nature of Mankind. The goal of theology is knowledge about the nature of God. Epistemology applied to theology refers to how we know what we know about the nature of God. Epistemology applied to psychology refers to how we know what we know about the nature of Mankind. Got it?

The Development of Modern Psychology: View of Knowledge – Faith/Science Dichotomy

Many believe that a Christian worldview and science are inherently in conflict. Many believe that the Bible has no place in science and that science has nothing to do with the Bible. In other words, some believe there is a faith/science dichotomy. That belief is evident by extension in the belief in a faith/psychology dichotomy. Some historians incorrectly make a case that the Church systematically fought every new scientific idea when in fact, science (and by extension, psychology) was born of the Christian worldview.

The historical Christian beliefs, traceable to Augustine, that God created a real, orderly, and rational world, that Mankind was created capable of knowing truth, and that God is immutable, set the stage for modern science. The historical Christian approach to science (though not without exception) was that reality is a unified whole and that there is no separation of science from faith. All of God's creation was to be discovered and enjoyed. The Christian fathers of modern science were not surprised to discover truths about the universe on the basis of reason. They saw science as a tool to discover God's mind, to explore His creation, to discover how God operates in natural processes, and to understand Mankind made in His image. Pascal, Bacon, Newton, and Galileo explored God's creation and then tested their ideas with science. Christians today should not be surprised or conflicted to discover "truths" of nature through science and reason and should reject the idea that a Christian worldview and science are inherent enemies.

To dichotomize "science" from "faith" destroys true science and marginalizes true faith. This text presumes that true psychology and Christianity are also complimentary. Work backwards. If there is no inherent dichotomy between faith and science, what is the source of the widespread and virulent anti-science and anti-psychology sentiment among some Christians? The real conflict is not between faith and science or between faith and psychology. The real conflict boils down to these epistemological questions:

- Is Scripture the only source of truth about the world (and by extension about Mankind)?
- Is Scripture the ultimate source of truth about the world (and by extension about Mankind)?
- Is Scripture a source of truth at all?
- What is the value of general (natural) revelation to our understanding of the nature of Mankind?

For further study:

Galileo Galilei was one of the greatest of scientists of all time. The Church's response to the theory of heliocentricity (the earth orbits the sun), developed by Copernicus and confirmed by Galileo, is often cited as evidence of Christendom's opposition to science. Read this article for the Catholic Church's position on the "Galileo controversy."

http://www.catholic.com/library/galileo_controversy.asp

The Development of Modern Psychology: View of Knowledge - All Truth is God's Truth

The warning in Colossians 2:8 to "Beware lest any man spoil you through philosophy and vain deceit, after the tradition of men, after the rudiments of the world, and not after Christ" is wise counsel for the Christian studying psychology (or for that matter, any academic discipline). St. Augustine, who said "All truth is God's Truth" and Justin Martyr, who concluded that, "whatever things were rightly said by any man belong to us Christians," should give pause to anyone who would reject psychology outright. The Christian worldview maintains that God reveals Himself in nature, in the Bible, and in Jesus Christ and that Truth is found in the agreement between God and His creation. Mankind can know truth about God and about creation because God has revealed Himself and given us the ability to understand. The Christian worldview presupposes that God's revelation is the source of all Truth and the comprehensive framework of reality. Though God has revealed Himself, He has not chosen to reveal all Truth. Though we were created with the capacity to understand, God's purposes are too big, our minds are too small, and our capacity for understanding is marred by sin.

The Development of Modern Psychology: View of Knowledge – General and Natural Revelation

God's revelation takes two forms, general (natural) revelation and special revelation. A Christian approach to the study of psychology must therefore rest on the assumption that God reveals psychological truths through both special and natural revelation. Natural revelation refers to truths revealed through observations of the world. We discover natural revelation by observing Creation, scientific (empirical) investigation, logic, and the study of history (any technique apart from reading the Bible or the working of the Holy Spirit). Special revelation refers to Biblical details about God's character, His purpose, His plan for Mankind, and our relationship with Him. Special revelation refers to God's works in history and the work of the Holy Spirit in humanity. Through the Bible God reveals all we need to know about His character and purpose. Theology focuses primarily on special revelation. Psychology focuses primarily on natural revelation. What scientists call "nature" is in reality God's creation.

Because all Truth comes from God, natural and special revelation are each part of an overarching and non-contradictory whole. When we understand that natural and special revelation are ultimately all encompassing and completely harmonious, Christians can be in awe of what has been revealed while seeking to discover what has not. It is science's purpose to better understand natural revelation. It is psychology's purpose to better understand natural revelation related to the nature of Mankind. If Truth is a unified whole and there is no inherent faith/science dichotomy, true science and true faith must agree. If Truth is a unified whole, natural revelation cannot contradict special revelation. The appearance of a contradiction is only an appearance. In terms of psychology, the appearance of a contradiction is the result of bad data (inadequate methodology, sampling, or replication), bad interpretation, or bad theology.

The role of natural revelation in the study of Mankind troubles many Christians. The role of special revelation in psychology troubles many psychologists. Some Christians believe that there is nothing that modern psychology can contribute to our understanding of Mankind. In other words, because God created us, only the Bible can explain us and there is no room for natural revelation about Mankind. That belief has some merit in light of the

Apostle Paul's teaching that there is wisdom that the unregenerate cannot understand (1 Corinthians 2:13-14). To cite Paul's warning as evidence that Christians should reject psychology, however, requires one to limit the value of natural revelation or to apply it unequally across creation. If indeed there is nothing that psychology can contribute to our understanding of Mankind, we must reconcile that with the fact that the Bible appears not to address all psychological issues and that the Bible appears to instruct us to use natural revelation.

This text presumes that because special and natural revelation cannot ultimately conflict, valid psychological data will fit with a Christian worldview. A Christian approach to psychology must recognize the value of all of God's revelation, special and natural. Special revelation provides a context or framework in which science can clarify and illuminate Biblical Truths. The error of Christians who limit God's communicative power about the nature of Mankind exclusively to the Bible is similar to the error of modern psychologists who discount the Bible's psychological insights.

The Development of Modern Psychology: View of Knowledge – Empiricism

Empiricism (also known as Positivism or Logical Positivism) asserts that the only valid foci of scientific inquiry are those things that can be known and measured by experience and observation. Empiricism, applied to psychology, limits psychology's focus to measurable and observable phenomena. Empiricism contends that experience is the ultimate source of all knowledge. The scientific method is empiricism's mode of operation. While logic and reason are a part of the process, empirical "truth" must ultimately come through the senses, controlled experimentation, and replication. As discussed previously, early modern psychology claimed the status of a natural science, distanced itself from philosophy, and claimed that the concepts of the mind, soul, and spirit were unscientific and outside the realm of science. All unobservable or un-replicable psychological phenomena were outside the realm of empirical psychology.

In the study of the natural world, empirical science is widely accepted and has produced a tremendous body of valuable research. Its value to the study of psychology is much less clear. Many of the characteristics of Mankind are intangible and cannot be measured or observed. A psychology that leaves out love, honor, faith, the spirit, and the soul is rightfully seen by many Christians as trivial. Strict empiricism, though appropriate to the study of Mankind's "creatureliness" reveals only sterile facts void of any meaningful contribution to what it means to be human. Difficulties applying empirical methods to psychological research (e.g. inability to control variables, bias, placebo effects) have led some to argue that psychology does not fit the definition of a true science and to challenge its reliance on the scientific method. Despite the shortcomings of strict empiricism, it continues as the dominant approach to psychological research.

The error of Christians who limit God's communicative power about the nature of Mankind exclusively to the Bible is similar to the error of modern psychologists who discount the Bible's psychological insights. So too, the error of the psychologist who relies solely on empirical methods is similar to the error of the Christian who discounts the value of experimentation. Empirical research is implied in Moses' admonition of 3,000 years ago: "When a prophet speaks in the name of the Lord, if the thing follow not, nor come to pass, that is the thing which the LORD hath not spoken" (Deuteronomy 18:22). In a spirit of humility, Christians studying psychology must be willing to put their scripturally informed knowledge about the nature of Mankind to the empirical test and be willing to view psychological science under the light of Scripture. God's Truth will survive experimental confirmation.

The Development of Modern Psychology: View of Knowledge – Bias and the Noetic Effect of Sin

A major goal of research in psychology is to control bias and minimize the influence of personal values and assumptions. The goal is worthy but probably unattainable. The psychologist and the Christian are both influenced by their underlying worldview. Psychologists try to eliminate that influence with methodological controls, but it is increasingly understood that scientific endeavors are inherently value-laden. Despite research indicating that research results often reflect the values of the researcher, many in psychology claim the discipline is value and bias-free. Similarly, many in Christendom believe that their personal interpretations of Biblical Truths are absolute and unambiguous. The fallacy of that belief is illustrated by the fact that though the Bible contains the infallible Word of God, Christian denominations debate (sometimes harshly) mutually contradictory doctrinal fine points.

A Christian worldview includes an acknowledgement of the effect of sin on our thinking (**the noetic effect of sin**). We know that what we know (about psychology and theology) is limited and impaired by sin (Romans 8:20-21; 1 Corinthians 13:12). Our personal bias and depravity should cause us to maintain a

> Assignment 4.3:
>
> Define: Total depravity

sense of humility and hold our conclusions tentatively. Confidence in the God of Truth allows us, without fear, to hold our conclusions tentatively.

For further study:

Read How Sin Affects Scholarship: A New Model by Stephen K. Moroney at:
http://www.asa3.org/ASA/topics/ethics/CSRSpring-1999Moroney.html

God's standards of right and wrong are "written on the human heart."

Chapter 5

A Christian worldview recognizes that there are built-in and universal moral absolutes that guide all human behavior. Modern academic psychology's perspective on the nature of right and wrong is best described as "moral relativism." In psychology, moral relativism assumes that human urges and impulses are the result of evolutionary processes and are "right" and beneficial. Repressive or restraining religious "traditions" are " wrong." This chapter begins with a comparison of the Christian and psychological view of right and wrong and concludes with a similar comparison of the views of the causes of and cures for mental pain.

The Development of Modern Psychology: View of Right and Wrong – Moral Relativism

Moral relativism is the application of a naturalistic worldview to ethics and personal responsibility. According to a Christian worldview, we are sinful by nature and choice, yet we are personally responsible for our actions. The Christian view stands in stark contrast to the view that sees man as inherently good that denies absolute moral standards, and does not hold people responsible for their behavior.

Approaches to sex education illustrate the difference between a theistic view and a morally relativistic view. Modern psychology describes sexuality in strictly biological terms and minimizes the importance of morality, religion, and personal responsibility. That approach is the antithesis of religious instruction that *defines* "normal" sexual relationships in terms of moral principles.

View of the causes of and cures for mental pain

One's perspective on sin, responsibility, and moral absolutes has huge implications for one's view of the causes of and cures for mental pain. No topic in psychology comes closer to the core of Mankind and to the heart of the Gospel message of sin and redemption than counseling psychology. Christians generally do not dispute the more basic observations of psychology. Psychologists' research on sensation and perception, testing, memory, and countless other topics are far from our "core" and clearly not the focus of Scripture. The more complex aspects of Mankind, the "human condition," our sin nature, salvation, restoration, and sanctification, however, are at the heart of the Gospel message. What it means to be "whole" is the essence of humanity and a primary focus of Scripture. As you might predict, the gravity of the subject matter contributes to tremendous disagreement in Christendom about the proper role (if any) of modern counseling psychology in the lives of Christians and non-Christians. For the Christian studying psychology, the nature and importance of the issues require great caution. For the Christian who plans to serve God in a career in mental health care, an in-depth and Spirit-informed theology is crucial.

Some of the key questions with which Christian psychologists, pastoral counselors, and theologians wrestle are:

- Does the experience of mental pain and suffering constitute a mental "illness?"
- Are mental illnesses best understood as the result of disunity with God, chemical imbalances, trauma and life experiences, or some combination?
- Are mental illnesses best treated from a spiritual or a medical perspective?
- Can unregenerate psychologists, using empirical methods, contribute anything to a Christian understanding of mental illness?
- Can the techniques developed by modern psychology contribute to a Christian approach to counseling?
- Can Christians safely borrow techniques from modern psychology to help those in mental pain?
- Can modern therapeutic techniques be detached from their underlying un-Christian worldview assumptions?
- Has the Church lost confidence in the power of the Gospel to heal?
- How do we explain the successes of secular therapeutic techniques at helping Christians and non-Christians alike?

One's worldview determines how one defines, evaluates the causes of, and treats mental illness. Some deny the existence of mental illnesses. Some explain mental illnesses in terms of sinful attitudes and behavior, and some, as has been the case for centuries, explain mental illness in terms of demonic activity. The predominant explanations from modern psychology are biological and social. Others suggest heredity, infections, brain defects or injury, substance abuse, and environmental toxins. Still others suggest smoking, refined sugar, and household cats cause or trigger mental illness.

> **Assignment 5.3**
>
> Read *The Myth of Mental Illness* by Dr. Thomas Szasz at:
>
> http://psychclassics.yorku.ca/Szasz/myth.htm
>
> Read about Drapetomania at
>
> http://en.wikipedia.org/wiki/Drapetomania

This text suggests that the symptoms and behaviors commonly referred to as mental illnesses are complex problems with a mixture of biological, social, and spiritual components. This text also suggests that the risk to Christians studying psychology is in accepting explanations that ignore, deny, or minimize the spiritual (including the demonic). A Christian worldview presupposes that when we are separated from God in an unregenerate state, we are by definition abnormal. A Christian worldview sees the "sin problem" as the foundational starting point for dealing with all problems of living, including mental illness. Modern psychology's atheistic assumptions, by definition, deny the influence of the demonic, but a

Christian worldview recognizes that demonic influences may account for some "mental illness."

View of the cause of and cures for mental pain: Sin

Neurobiology, heredity, infections, refined sugar, and house cats may contribute to mental illness, but one's spiritual condition is crucial to sound mental health. A Christian worldview emphasizes sin as the primary (if not exclusive) cause of mental and emotional pain; modern psychology attributes it to anything but sin.

> **Assignment 5.4**
>
> Read *What is Nouthetic Counseling* by Dr. Jay Adams at http://www.nouthetic.org/

A Christian view also differs from modern psychology's view in its recognition that guilt, pain, and suffering are tools at God's disposal as He conforms us to Christ's image. Jesus was a "man of sorrows." It is noteworthy that many in Christendom share modern psychology's view that emotional pain must be avoided at all costs. A "feel good" gospel has much in common with modern psychology's selfism (see Chapter 3).

View of the causes of and cures for mental pain: Counseling

In one sense, counseling has been around for all of human history. The Old Testament gives examples of forms of counseling (encouraging, guiding, confronting, and advising one another). In the New Testament Jesus is called the "Wonderful Counselor" and in the early Church the Apostles cared for people's physical, spiritual, and psychological needs. In another sense, counseling is very young.

In the early 20th century there was a major split in the North American Church. In addition to doctrinal differences, "liberal" churches adopted techniques from modern psychology to minister to people's psychological needs. The work of Anton Boisen led to the development of "Pastoral Counseling" as a distinct approach to the care of souls. "Liberal" pastoral counselors borrowed from modern psychology and interpreted mental problems more in terms of "sickness" than sin. "Conservative" churches focused more on sin and salvation.

Today, the extent to which Christians disagree over psychology is often a function of differences in "conservative" and "liberal" Christian worldviews.

For further study:

Read the biography of Anton Boisen at http://www.acpe.edu/networks/boisen_bio.htm

Read a history of the Association for Clinical Pastoral Education at http://www.acpe.edu/cpehistory.htm

---

As you might guess, "conservatives" criticize those who adopt the practices of modern psychology for "losing their Biblical moorings." Hobart Mowrer (1961) asked, "has evangelical religion sold its birthright for a mess of psychological pottage?" On the other hand, the "liberal" Church suggests that "conservatives" fail to minister to the "whole" person and that the "just pray harder" approach is less effective than the techniques developed by modern psychology. Some attribute the growth of secular approaches to counseling to a failure of the Church. The Church sometimes fails to minister to emotional needs and many who seek help do not look to the Church for that help (Beck, 2005).

This text suggested that the symptoms and behaviors commonly referred to as mental illnesses are complex problems with a mixture of biological, social, and spiritual components. It also suggests that the care for those problems is equally complex and multi-faceted. Psychological healing, like physical healing, is the work God. As God uses medical doctors in physical healing, He uses pastors, counselors, and laypeople to encourage, help, and counsel one another. Those with a special spiritual gift practice forms of "Christian" or "Biblical" counseling. But there is no single widely accepted approach to Biblical or Christian counseling. There is wide agreement however that the process should include the Gospel message of salvation and the results should be alignment with Jesus' self-concept, relationships, thoughts, emotions, behavior, and will. Jesus Christ is the core of true Christian counseling and the model of mental health.

View of the causes of and cures for mental pain: Criticisms of Counseling

Christian criticism of counseling (anti-psychology) take four general positions:

- Modern psychology's approach to counseling is inconsistent with the practice of Christianity.
- The science of psychology presents a model of human nature that is in direct competition with Christianity.
- Using techniques from modern psychology is tantamount to declaring the Bible inadequate.
- Integrating psychology and Christianity is not possible.

The expressions of those criticisms take many forms, such as:

- Psychology is "the most deadly form of modernism ever to confront the church."
- Psychology is a religious wolf in pseudoscientific clothing.
- Psychology is an idolatrous, heretical, and ungodly rival religion that places Christians at risk of spiritual deception and demonic attack.
- Psychology is better described as "psycho quackery" and "psycho heresy."
- Psychology is part of the "the great seduction in preparation for the antichrist."
- Psychology is Satan's substitute for Biblical remedies.
- The Bible is the sole source of information about Man's nature, behavior, thoughts, and emotions.

> **Assignment 5.5**
> **Read Psychology and the Doctrines of Devils at:**
> http://www.thebereancall.org/node/2431

- The Bible is sufficient to deal with all problems of living including "psychiatric" conditions.
- Psychotherapy is questionable at best, detrimental at worst, and a spiritual counterfeit at least.
- There are no valid scientific reasons for using professional psychotherapy by believers or unbelievers.
- The psychological way of understanding and changing people is condemned by the Bible.
- Psychology is a rival religion.
- Spiritual deception and demonic attack are possible consequences of involvement in psychology.

The responses to those criticisms include:

- Anti-psychology arguments are shallow and illogical, unsophisticated, and reckless.
- Anti-psychology arguments are contorted and contrived and use outdated material.
- The anti-psychology position fails to acknowledge that the Bible appears to instruct man to use extra-biblical personal observation, rational discourse, and experience as guides.
- It does not recognize the value of natural revelation and assumes that there is no natural revelation about the nature of Mankind that can be discovered by a non-Christian.
- The position requires a belief that by "probing the unfathomed depth and breadth of Scripture" the Bible addresses problems like anorexia and schizophrenia.
- The position leads to inevitable cultural isolation and irrelevance.
- The position unevenly applies criticisms to psychology but not to other disciplines (medicine, economics, or physics).

The criticisms of counseling psychology are not limited to Christians. Secular criticisms of counseling psychology include:

- Untreated people recover at about the same rate as those in treatment.
- Most types of counseling are equally ineffective.
- Psychology is just common sense.
- It is preoccupied with sex.
- Psychologists are unstable people who cannot solve their own problems or control their unruly children.
- Psychology invades privacy and restricts individual freedom.
- Psychology uses powerful tools for controlling human behavior.
- Psychology is irrelevant and has discovered few laws of behavior.
- The methodology is flawed and not really a science.
- Psychology is too fragmented and overly specialized.
- "Mental illness" is a metaphor for disapproved thoughts, feelings, and behaviors.

Assignment 5.6

Download and read "The End of Christian Psychology" at:

http://www.psychoheresy-aware.org/ECPbk_online.html Read pages 3-9

Assignment 5.7

Read the "Welcome" page of the Society for Christian Psychology at:
http://christianpsych.org/home.php

Read the "Mission Statement of the Society for Christian Psychology" by
clicking the link "About SCP" or go to
http://christianpsych.org/wp_scp/?page_id=15

The key point is that psychology was not discovered, invented, or created in the 19th century; it only became "modern."

Psychology is not new. It is old and new. Sigmund Freud did not invent psychology and his work did not signal the beginning of the study of psychology. Though most histories date the beginning of psychology to 1879 with the founding of Wilhelm Wundt's psychological laboratory in Germany, Wundt did not invent psychology nor did his work signal its beginning. Psychology is new in the sense that the first use of controlled psychological experimentation does date to Wundt's but it is old in the sense that there was psychological theorizing and research centuries prior. Modern scientific psychology, as an academic discipline, independent from philosophy, does date to the mid 19th century. But if we accept that psychology is the study of the soul, the mind, and the relationship of life and mind to the functions of the body, we discover that great thinkers and theologians throughout history considered psychological questions long before the "science" of psychology appeared. It should be no surprise learn that Christian and non-Christian thinkers throughout history have thought deeply about psychology. In fact, in the years before the establishment of psychology as a distinct discipline, the topic of Mankind's mind was well covered by religion, philosophy, and literature. As psychological thinking predates modern psychology, so too does the tension and debate between psychology and a Christian worldview.

The key point is that psychology was not discovered, invented, or created in the 19th century; it only became "modern." If psychology were only new, Christians would be well advised to avoid the entire discipline. If it is old and new, Christians have a duty to influence the new with the spirit of the old.

Modern Psychology: History

College-level introductory psychology courses may address ancient theories about the nature of Mankind ("old psychology"), but those theories will probably be presented as something other than true scientific psychology. If psychology is "the branch of philosophy that studies the soul, the mind, and the relationship of life and mind to the functions of the body psychology," then old psychology is truly psychology too. Consider that:

- Around 640 B. C. **Psamtik**, the King of Egypt, conducted psychological experiments on language acquisition.
- The Greek philosopher **Thales** (circa 600 B. C.) suggested that being "happy" meant being "healthy in body, resourceful in soul and of a readily teachable nature."
- Around 450 B.C. **Protagoras** suggested that the "mind" was the seat of truth and knowledge.
- In the late fifth and early fourth centuries B.C., **Socrates** and then **Plato,** applied reason to philosophical questions about the nature of Mankind.
- **Democritus**, 460-370 BCE, suggested that soul consisted of atoms of fire and that our senses were able to sense and interpret atoms striking the body. Democritus suggested that that happiness was the result of an even temperament.
- **Epicurus**, 341-271 B. C., believed that pleasure and tranquility was the purpose of all human behavior. Tranquility and pleasure came by ridding one's self of the fear of death.
- **Zeno of Elea**, 336 - 264 B.C., taught that peace could only be found through controlling emotions.
- Around 120 A. D., **Galen** developed a theory of personalities and classified emotions.
- The early Christian Church, as described in the New Testament, studied the care and healing of the soul (pastoral care and counseling).
- Around 200 A. D. **Tertullian** produced De Anima (On the Soul) the first Christian writing in psychology outside of the New Testament.
- In the 4th century A.D. **Augustine, Bishop of Hippo**, infused philosophy with Christian doctrine and wrote about love, memory, mental illumination, wisdom, and volition.
- **Cassian, Gregory of Nyssa**, and **Gregory the Great, Thomas Aquinas, Teresa of Avila, John of the Cross, Giovanni Vico, John Locke, Bishop George Berkeley, Thomas Reid, Bishop Joseph Butler, Gottfried Leibniz**, and **Blaise Pascal**, contributed to Christian psychology long before founding of modern psychology,
- **Martin Luther** and **John Calvin** reflected on grace, knowledge, faith, and the nature of life
- In 1247 the Bethlehem Royal Hospital (**Bedlam**), began 750 years of caring for people with mental disorders.
- In 1506, **Marco Marulic** first used the term psychology (psichiologia).
- In 1649, **René Descartes** suggested a separation of body and soul (dualism) in *Passions of the Soul*. Descartes divided behavior into two classes — voluntary and involuntary. Voluntary behavior was

governed by the mind and was thought to be non-mechanical and non-physical. Involuntary behavior was thought to be completely mechanical and physical (a function of "animal spirits" which traveled along nerves in what came to be known as a "reflex arc"). According to Descartes, the reflex arc accounted for all animal behavior and parts of human behavior. Before Descartes, the suggestion that human behavior had anything in common with animal behavior would have been viewed as ludicrous.

- In 1651, **Thomas Hobbes** published the *Leviathan* that, though primarily a political work, examined the nature Mankind's motivations. Like Descartes, Hobbes saw voluntary behavior as a function of the mind. Unlike Descartes, Hobbes believed that the functioning of the mind was also subject to mechanical laws. According to Hobbes, the sole objective of human behavior was the avoidance of pain and the pursuit of pleasure.

- In 1690, **John Locke** wrote *An Essay Concerning Human Understanding* exploring the nature of the self.

- **George Berkeley**, (1685-1753), suggested that everything that exists depends on the mind for its existence.

- **David Hume**, 1711-1776, questioned ideas about the "self," our knowledge of the external world, free will and determinism, and meaning.

- **Immanuel Kant**, 1724-1804, an influential German philosopher published *Critique of Pure Reason* which addressed epistemology, ethics, aesthetics, and teleology. Kant wrote of our cognitive ability to give meaning and structure to the world.

- **Soren Kierkegaard**, 1813-1855, who considered himself a Christian psychologist, produced profound psychological work on anxiety, despair, melancholy, sacrifice, and love.

For further reading, review the material at:

The Christian Classics Ethereal Library at http://www.ccel.org/
Classics in the History of Psychology at http://psychclassics.yorku.ca/
A Brief Survey of the History of Biblical Psychology at
http://www.mattcohn.net/history.html

For further study:

Democritus: http://www.iep.utm.edu/d/democrit.htm

Epicurus: http://www.iep.utm.edu/e/epicur.htm

Stoicism: http://plato.stanford.edu/entries/stoicism/

Galen: http://www.iep.utm.edu/g/galen.htm

Bedlem: http://www.newadvent.org/cathen/02387b.htm

Marulic (The Author of the Term "Psychology)
http://psychclassics.yorku.ca/Krstic/marulic.htm

Descartes:
http://net.cgu.edu/philosophy/descartes/Passions_Letters.html

Hobbes:
http://etext.library.adelaide.edu.au/h/hobbes/thomas/h68l/

Locke:
http://psychology.okstate.edu/museum/history/undrstnd.txt

Berkley: http://psychclassics.yorku.ca/Berkeley/vision.htm

Hume: http://etext.library.adelaide.edu.au/h/hume/david/h92e/

Kant: http://www.hkbu.edu.hk/~ppp/cpr/toc.html

Modern psychology, as a "new" natural science, began moving away from philosophy in the early 19th century. New "schools of thought" described new perspectives on the nature of Mankind. Each new school of thought re-defined the "proper" focus of psychology. Each new school of thought (structuralist, functionalist, psychoanalytic, behaviorist, humanist, and cognitive) redefined the nature of Mankind and mental processes, defined the direction of psychological inquiry, and moved psychology progressively further from it philosophical roots.

The **structuralists** viewed mental experiences as "structures" built from simple mental states much like as complex chemical compounds are composed of simpler chemical elements. **Functionalists** explored the ways mental experiences help people adjust to their environment. **Behaviorists** focused on observable behavior and **psychoanalysts** or **dynamic** psychologists emphasized the importance of unconscious processes.

Humanists emphasized the content of our conscious thoughts and feelings and our ability to influence the environment and the **cognitivists** examined the processes by which we perceive, solve problems, remember, and think.

Modern Psychology: Structuralists

Franz Joseph Gall and **Dr. Charles Bell** influenced the prominent structuralists, **William Wundt**, **Edward Titchener**, and **Gustav Theodor Fechner**.

Dr. Charles Bell (1774-1842) discovered that nerves travel from the brain to the organs and support both sensory and motor functions. **Dr. Franz Gall** (1758-1828), an anatomist and physiologist, was instrumental in locating the source of mental activity in the brain. Dr. Gall also founded phrenology. **Phrenology,** now discredited,

> For further study:
>
> Read Gustav Theodor Fechner's *Elements of Psychophysics* at http://psychclassics.yorku.ca/Fechner/

> Bell's palsy, named for Dr. Charles Bell who first described the condition, is a weakness or paralysis in the muscles controlling expressions on one side of the face. Bell's palsy is caused by damage to one of a pair of facial nerves running beneath each ear to the muscles in the face.

suggested that the shape of the skull indicated a person's character and personality. Dr. Gall attributed various mental functions and personality traits to specific parts of the brain and he believed that the shape of the skull mirrored the shape of the brain. He attributed various mental characteristics to more or less brain matter in corresponding parts of the brain. If one portion of the brain was better developed (bigger), Gall believed that the skull would reflect that difference. Gall believed that good memory was associated with prominent eyes (the occipital lobe) and that one's "individuality" was apparent by the shape of the skull above the bridge of the nose. Gall believed that close examination of the skull enabled him to identify those with special abilities in the arts. It is interesting that Gall's work on the anatomy of the brain was condemned as heretical for claiming that the "mind," created by God, should have a seat in brain matter.

> The expression, "You ought to have your head examined" goes back to phrenologists, who literally examined people's heads in order to analyze their personalities.

Gustav Theodor Fechner (1801 – 1887), who shares the title of father of modern experimental psychology with his successor William Wundt, used instruments to answer questions like; "What is the smallest unit of energy (e.g. light or sound) a person can perceive?" Fechner's work demonstrated that scientific procedures could be applied to some mental phenomena. Fechner's use of experimental methods were precise and methodical and ushered in experimentation as the primary tool of modern scientific psychology.

Wilhelm Wundt (1832 – 1920), known by many as the father of modern psychology, also used experimental methods for his research into the components of consciousness. Wundt studied the time it took subjects to react to stimulation like sounds and sights. Wundt and Fechner believed that mental activity could be broken down into fundamental components (**structuralism**). Molecular-level advances in chemistry and physics encouraged the structuralists to look for the fundamental components of which complex mental processes were thought to be composed.

Edward B. Titchener (1867 – 1927), who trained under Wundt, published *Experimental Psychology: A Manual of Laboratory Practice*, the first guide for conducting psychological research. Titchener, who coined the term **structuralism**, examined sensations, attention, perception and a host of other mental phenomena. Though a structuralist, Titchener recognized that the functional aspects of mental processes were relevant and important topics for study.

Modern Psychology: Functionalists

Functionalists explored mental processes in terms of their purpose or function. The functionalists were influenced by the work of **Herbert Spencer** and **Charles Darwin**. An outgrowth of Darwin and Spencer's evolutionary theories, functionalism focused on the adaptive (evolutionary) purpose of the brain, mind, and behavior rather than structures. **William James** and **Edward Thorndike** were influential functionalists.

Herbert Spencer (1820 – 1903), who coined the phrase "**survival of the fittest**," published two volumes of *Principles of Psychology*. Spencer used genetic and evolutionary principles to describe mental processes. Spencer suggested that some behaviors produced pleasurable outcomes (or outcomes which reduced pain), which were more likely to be repeated. If a pleasurable outcome promoted survival (of the fittest), those behaviors would continue and pass to subsequent generations. Likewise, **Charles Darwin's** *The Origin of Species* set the stage for descriptions of complex mental processes as collections of simpler underlying processes, each with a development and purpose best explained by evolution. Spencer and Darwin set the stage for psychology's full departure from philosophy and religion.

By the late 19th century, Darwin's ideas about evolution were well known to scientists, and psychologists began to propose theories explaining mental processes in terms of evolutionary forces. **Williams James** (1842 – 1910), applied Darwin's theory to psychology and suggested that our mental processes and consciousness evolved because they were was beneficial for survival. James was an influential and prolific theorist and viewed the mind in terms of its function (**functionalism**). James, known as the father of American psychology, described mental processes, not in terms of components (structuralism), but in terms of the processes' purpose.

Edward Thorndike (1874 – 1949) was both a functionalist and an early behaviorist. Thorndike's major contribution to the study of psychology was the application of functionalism to learning in animals. He was very influential in understanding learning and paved the way for **B. F. Skinner**, **John Watson**, and the development of **behavioral psychology**. Thorndike constructed "puzzle boxes" in which, when rewarded for a particular response, animals learned to repeat that response. If not rewarded, the responses gradually disappeared. Thorndike described animal behavior in terms of functions and, as a preview of behaviorism, concluded that animals learn solely by trial and error.

For further study:

Read Thordinke's *Animal Intelligence; A Note on the Psychology of Fishes* (Chapter IV) at
http://psychclassics.yorku.ca/Thorndike/Animal/fish.htm

Read a biography of Thorndike at
http://www.muskingum.edu/~psych/psycweb/history/thorndike.htm

---

Modern Psychology: Behaviorism

Chapter 9 covers the principles of behaviorism in more detail. In terms of the history of psychology, behaviorism represented psychology's attempt to remove **introspection** (subjects' self reporting of mental activity) and subjective experience as the focus of psychological research. Behavior theory sought to explain the laws that relate past experiences to future action. Behaviorism views environmental events as the key determinant of behavior. In 1905, **William McDougall** first defined psychology as "the study of behavior" and in 1912, **John B. Watson** (1878-

1958) coined the word **"behaviorism"** as an approach to psychology in which observable behaviors were the only appropriate topic of psychological research. Internal mental states and processes were thought too subjective for scientific study. Watson's assertion that "there was no dividing line between man and brute" (Watson, 1913) typified the evolutionary thought in American psychology. Behaviorists hoped they could explain and control human behavior.

> Give me a dozen healthy infants, well-formed, and my own special world to bring them up in, and I'll guarantee to take any one at random and train him to become any type of specialist I might select-doctor, lawyer, artist, merchant-chief, and yes, beggerman and thief (J. B. Watson, 1913).

The most well known behaviorist is B. F. Skinner (1904-1990). Recognizing that Pavlov's classical conditioning principles were insufficient to explain all learning, Skinner described "operant conditioning" as the process by which humans and animals learn. Skinner's "radical behaviorism" held that freedom is an illusion and that Mankind does not have the ability to transcend environmental influences. Skinner saw humans as closed cause-and-effect systems. Since Skinner, behavioral psychologists have developed countless behavior modification procedures for training animals and modifying human behavior.

Modern Psychology: Freud

From the perspective of the history of psychology, Freudian psychoanalysis or the **psychoanalytic** school of psychology was in many ways the polar opposite of behaviorism.

Sigmund Freud, a neurologist and psychiatrist, commonly known as the "father of psychoanalysis," is without question the most influential and controversial figure in psychology. Though important as an influence, his work was not supported by research and has value today primarily for a historical perspective of psychology's development. Sigmund Freud's psychoanalytic approach emphasized the importance of unconscious mental processes. According to Freud, innate instincts and unconscious processes are key to understanding Mankind. According to Freudian theory, the unconscious is a battlefield where animal instincts (mainly sex and aggression) war with societal pressures to control those impulses.

Modern Psychology: Humanism

By the 1970s, behaviorism and psychoanalysis were losing favor. Dissatisfaction with the two primary theories (behaviorism and Freudianism) led to psychology's "third force" or **humanistic** psychology.

Humanist psychology asserts that we can be actualized (reach our full potential) in an accepting and nonjudgmental environment. Humanist psychologists (most notably **Abraham Maslow** and **Carl Rogers**) described Mankind in terms of human potential, needs, self identify, inner fulfillment, and emotions. The humanists focus less on behavior and subconscious influences and more on meaning and purpose. Though humanistic psychologists "respect and value" religious feelings, humanistic psychology, like secular humanism, denies the objective reality of God and therefore conflicts fundamentally with a Christian worldview. The importance humanistic psychology placed on personal growth and potential is widely accepted by many psychologists today.

Modern Psychology: Cognitivism

Psychology today is dominated by cognitive psychology and neuro-biology. Cognitive psychology emphasizes the ways we process information. Cognitive psychology has its roots in structuralism but re-emerged in the era of computers. Computers became a metaphor for the brain's capacity to process information. Though computer programs appear very complex, they can be reduced to very simple underlying structures (ones and zeros). Cognitivism is the foundation for much of modern psychotherapy and counseling. The brain, like a computer, may need "re-programming" to correct errors in its "inputs and outputs."

Modern Psychology: Neuro-biology

Neuro-biology, also with roots in structuralism, describes behavior and mental processes in terms of the brain and the nervous system Advances in technology allow researchers to "see" brain structures and the biological processes involved in mental activity. Technology allows researchers to correlate any mental activity, from solving a problem to praying, to activity in specific parts of the brain. Advances in neuro-pharmacology allows researchers to use drugs to precisely affect brain functioning.

For further study: Review major figures in psychology at http://www.sparknotes.com/psychology/psych101/majorfigures/characters.html

For further study:

Annenberg Media, a unit of The Annenberg Foundation produced a series of videos available free (with registration) intended to advance teaching in all disciplines.

Discovering Psychology is a series of 26 half-hour introductory psychology video programs intended for high school and college classrooms.

The videos present an overview of historic and current theories of human behavior and provide an excellent opportunity for parents to expose their students to modern psychological material in the context of the homeschool. The videos are available at http://www.learner.org/resources/series138.html

Section II

In Section I we examined psychology from a worldview perspective. In Section II, we focus on psychology's content. Introductory psychology texts generally describe four purposes for psychological research.

- **Observe and describe** the brain, behavior, thoughts, learning, and emotions objectively and in detail.
- **Suggest meaning** (theories) to explain those observations and the factors that contribute to and influence what we observe.
- Use observations and theories to **predict** behavior.
- Develop techniques to **improve or otherwise change** behavior, thoughts, learning, and emotions.

Introductory psychology texts generally approach the content of psychology from five perspectives.

- The **biological** approach observes, explains, predicts, and improves in terms of biological structures and electro-chemical processes.
- The **behavioral** approach emphasizes the relationship between environmental influences and behavior.
- The **cognitive** approach emphasizes conscious thought processes. Cognition refers to perception, problem solving, memory, thinking, and any mental process that transforms sensory input.
- The **psychoanalytic** approach emphasizes unconscious processes.
- The **humanistic** approach emphasizes the influence of our thoughts, feelings, and experiences on the environment and emphasizes innate goodness and potential.

This text suggests a sixth approach to psychology's content.

- The **spiritual** approach recognizes that Mankind is both physical and spiritual. This text suggests that it is not possible to describe, explain, or change Mankind without reference to God in whose image we are created.

The human brain is a most unusual instrument of elegant and as yet unknown capacity. - Stuart Seaton

Modern Psychology: The Biological Components

The human nervous system is an incredibly complex and highly coordinated network. It has been described as the most complex structure in the known universe. Our brains are wonders of God's creation. Estimates of the number of nerve cells in a human brain range from 20 billion to a trillion. With each nerve connecting to many neighboring nerves, the complexity of the connections in the human brain is truly staggering.

The Bible does not mention the brain. The Bible mentions the heart, mind, blood, bowels, liver, and kidneys, but not the brain. For most of human history, the heart was thought to be the most important organ and the seat of the mind. The ancient Greeks thought the lungs contained the mind. Descartes thought the pineal gland was home to the mind. Around 400 B. C., Hippocrates suggested that the brain, not the heart, was the seat of the mind, but it was not until the 17th century that the importance of the brain's role in human thoughts and emotions gained wide acceptance. While anatomists debated which organ was the seat of the mind, philosophers and theologians debated and continue to debate parallel but deeper questions. Do we have a mind or soul that exists independent from the physical brain? Does the mind or soul reside in the brain? Is the mind material or spiritual? Is the mind more than the sum of the complex electro-chemical operations of brain?

The field of **psychobiology** (the study of the nervous system's structures and biochemical processes; also known as **neuropsychology** or **neurobiology**) is the most productive field of research in psychology and a predominant psychological "school of thought" today. Advances in technology allow scientists today to observe brain functioning at a level unthinkable a few years ago. Technological advances provide evidence suggesting that some phenomena, once thought to be the working of the immaterial mind, involve physical brain processes. New technology allows scientists to view the physical, electrical, and chemical process in the brain as we think, remember, dream, meditate, and pray. It is not surprising that research indicates that our experience of God, though a spiritual event, involves the brain. New technology has emboldened those who suggest that we do not have a spiritual (immaterial) component; that we are no more than complex biochemical processes operating in brain matter. Introductory psychology courses will likely present the concept of an immaterial "mind" as naïve and unscientific. While a Christian worldview is generally dualistic, introductory psychology courses will likely suggest that ALL mental experiences (including religious experience) are nothing more than brain functioning. To modern psychology, if the mind exists, it exists within the structures of the brain. Introductory psychology course focus **reductively** on brain structures and functions. Remember that reductionist assumptions are common in modern psychology. If Man is nothing more than a complex machine, then the brain is the central processing unit; complicated, but reducible to simpler underlying parts. Reductionism, applied to the brain, means that all brain activity (including love, hope, prayer, worship, etc) is ultimately nothing more than biochemical processes. This text suggests that we are both material and immaterial. Our brains and minds are distinct, but inextricably linked.

What does that mean for the Christian studying psychology? It requires us to be humble. We must humbly accept that the complexities of the human brain are such that we will likely never fully understand them. It allows us to be bold. The near-infinite complexity of the brain represents the single biggest "leap of faith" necessary to hold an evolutionary worldview. It requires us to be skeptical of the psychologist and the theologian who speak with certainty about the mind or the brain. We should marvel at the wonder of the brain. We should praise God for the gift inside our skulls. We must accept that God appears to have chosen to use the brain as a conduit through which our material and immaterial natures relate. While seeking greater understanding, we must accept that God's ways are greater than our understanding. We must be confident that if God chose to operate through brain processes, it does not diminish Him or us.

For further study:

Read *The Human Nervous System: Evidence of Intelligent Design [Part II]* by Brad Harrub, Ph.D. at
http://www.apologeticspress.org/articles/695

Read *Evidence for Intelligent Design from Biochemistry* by Michael J. Behe at http://www.arn.org/docs/behe/mb_idfrombiochemistry.htm

Read *Mind Life* by P. David Glanzer at
www.asa3.org/ASA/topics/PsychologyNeuroscience/PSCF6-01Glanzer.html

The Nervous System

Volumes have been written about the structure of the nervous system. An in-depth discussion of psychobiology is beyond the scope of this text. This text, like most introductory psychology courses, offers a simple overview of the brain and nervous system. The reader is cautioned that simple overviews miss the incredible wonder of the human nervous system.

The human nervous system consists of two systems; the **central nervous system (CNS)** and the **peripheral nervous system (PNS).** The **Central Nervous System** consists of the **brain** and the **spinal cord.** The **Peripheral Nervous System** consists of those nerves outside of the brain and the spinal cord. The peripheral nervous system, made up of the **somatic, autonomic,** and **enteric** systems, is the network of nerves traveling throughout the entire body.

The Brain

The living brain is pink and soft. It is shielded by the **skull,** cushioned and nourished in **cerebrospinal fluid,** and protected from toxins by the **blood-brain barrier.** The blood-brain barrier is a membrane that lets some substances from the blood into the brain but keeps out toxins. The spinal cord connects the brain with the body and transmits signals from the brain to the body and back again. It too is shielded by bone (the **spinal column**) and nourished in cerebrospinal fluid.

In the embryo, brain development begins as a tube of cells that rapidly develop into three distinct parts; the **forebrain, midbrain,** and **hindbrain.** Forebrain, midbrain, and hindbrain describe regions of the brain, each containing several brain structures. The forebrain consists of the **cerebrum, thalamus,** and **hypothalamus.** The midbrain (also known as the brainstem) consists of the **tectum** and **tegmentum.** The hindbrain consists of the **cerebellum, pons,** and **medulla.** This text examines three principal brain structures; the **cerebrum, cerebellum,** and **medulla.**

For further study:

View the Whole Brain Atlas Top 100 Brain Structures at
http://www.med.harvard.edu/AANLIB/cases/caseM/case.html

The Brain: Cerebrum

As the brain develops, it folds into deep wrinkles called **convolutions**. Convolutions allow more brain surface area to fit in the limited space of the skull. Convolutions continue to form and deepen for years after birth. The **cerebrum**, the largest and topmost part of the brain, makes up about two-thirds of brain matter. The cerebrum is associated with human intelligence and reasoning. The cerebrum's outermost layer, where most of the brain's cell bodies are packed, is called the **cerebral cortex**. The word **cortex** refers to the dense outer layer of any brain structure. The cerebral cortex appears gray when preserved (hence the term "**gray matter**"). Sections of the cerebrum are described as **hemispheres** and **lobes**. The **longitudinal sulcus**, a deep fissure, splits the brain down the middle into the left and right hemispheres. **Bilateral symmetry** refers to the left and right hemispheres

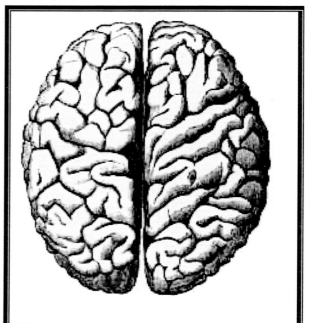

The left and right hemisphere of the cerebrum showing convolutions (folds) and the longitudinal sulcus (deep fissure dividing the cerebrum in half).

The Wada test (named for the neurologist who first performed the procedure) demonstrated that some mental processes are localized to the right or left hemisphere. The Wada test involves injecting an anesthetic into one brain hemisphere. While one hemisphere is anesthetized (asleep), the other remains awake and conscious. Researchers can interview the patients or have them perform tasks to determine which hemisphere control particular mental processes.

appearing as mirror images. The left and right hemispheres are connected by a dense bundle of fiber called the **corpus callosum**. The corpus callosum allows the two halves of the brain to communicate and is the only place where the two cerebral hemispheres are connected.

Hemispheric specialization refers to the different roles the hemispheres play in mental functioning. The fundamental hemispheric specialization has to do with controlling movement. In humans and most animals, each side of the brain controls the opposite (**contralateral**) side of the body. Similarly, touch receptors on the left side of the body transmit signals to the right hemisphere of the brain, while touch receptors on the right side of the body transmit signals to the left hemisphere

---

For further study:

Read about Roger Sperry's Split-Brain Operations at: http://nobelprize.org/educational_games/medicine/split-brain/background.html

---

Handedness

(left-handed or right-handed) is a function of the **dominance** of the opposite brain hemisphere. Generally, language is localized in

> **About 13% of the human population is naturally left-handed. For the other 87%, the right arm works better for skilled hand movements.**

the left hemisphere and spatial processing on the right. Though popular psychology often claims that hemispheric specialization plays a major role in a wide variety of psychological processes, most complex mental activity involves a mix of areas on both sides.

Other fissures divide sections of the cerebrum into **lobes** named for the parts of the skull under which they are located. As with hemispheric specialization, some mental activity is localized in specific lobes and some involves several. For example, visual processing is localized in the **occipital lobe** at the back of the brain. The occipital lobe collaborates with other brain structures in the

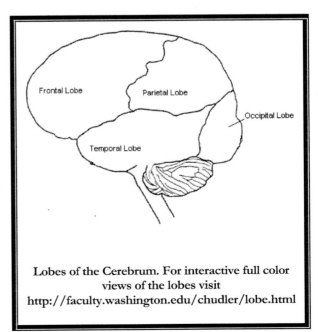

Lobes of the Cerebrum. For interactive full color views of the lobes visit http://faculty.washington.edu/chudler/lobe.html

formation of memory. The **parietal lobe** is the middle area of the brain. The parietal lobe is involved in spatial processing and in interpreting of our sense of touch. The **temporal lobes**, on the sides of the brain near the ears, are involved in hearing and collaborates with other parts of the brain in memory and emotion. The **frontal** lobe, in the front of the brain, is related to **executive functions** like attention, organization, planning, judgment, problem solving, and creativity.

The Brain: Cerebellum

The **cerebellum**, located under the cerebrum at the back of the skull, is the second largest brain structure. The cerebellum is often described as "the little brain" and assumed to be much older evolutionarily. The cerebellum is associated with hand-eye coordination, balance, motor related memory, and problem solving.

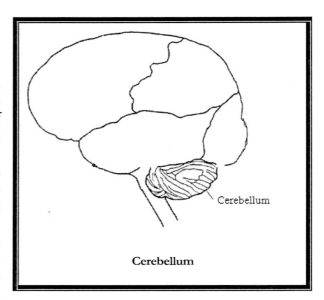

Cerebellum

Cerebellum

The Brain: Medulla

The **medulla**, or medulla oblongata, is part of the brain stem located at the top of the spinal cord. The medulla is responsible for many vital functions including breathing, temperature regulation, and some aspects of speech.

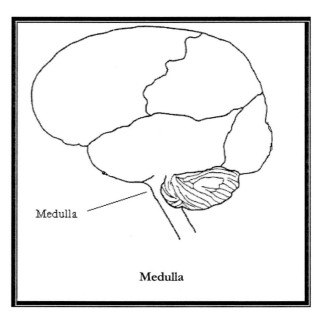

Medulla

Medulla

The theory of homology asserts that the presence of similar anatomical structures in different species is evidence of evolutionary processes. Many structures in the human brain are also present in animals, but the size and complexity of the human cerebrum is unique. Many introductory psychology courses claim that the brain structures humans share with animals are evidence of evolution. Brain structures associated with regulating reflexes (breathing, heart rate, appetite), common in humans and animals, are said to be "older" from an evolutionary perspective. The human cerebrum (especially the frontal lobe), unique to humans, is thought to be a recent evolutionary development.

The Brain and Behavior

To study the functioning of the brain and its relationship to behavior, researchers must use a living brain. Most of our knowledge about the relationship of the brain and behavior comes from the study of brain injuries, intentional destruction of brain tissue, brain stimulation, and brain imaging.

The Brain and Behavior: Brain Injury

Since the ancient Egyptians, brain injuries provided the bulk of the information about the relationship of the brain to behavior Researchers examined victims of brain injury to learn what the victims could and could not do to correlate behavior with the injured portion of the brain. Accidents (blunt trauma or punctures), tumors, oxygen deprivation, and strokes are examples of injuries to the brain.

Aphasias, disorders of speech due to brain injury, provided early researchers evidence of which portions of the brain are involved in language. The most well-known aphasias are **Broca's aphasia** and **Wernicke's aphasia**.

For further study of aphasias, visit the National Institute on Deafness and Other Communication Disorders at
http://www.nidcd.nih.gov/health/voice/aphasia.htm

A famous example of how of brain injuries led to knowledge about the brain is the case of Phineas P. Gage. Gage was a railway worker in Vermont in 1848. An accidental explosion blew a 43-inch, 13.5-pound rod completely through his head. The rod entered his skull under the cheek and traveled completely through his skull landing about 30 yards behind him. Even though part of his brain was destroyed, Mr. Gage never lost consciousness. The changes in Gage's personality suggested a relation between personality and the front parts of the brain.

Read the story of Phinehas P. Gage at
http://www.deakin.edu.au/hmnbs/psychology/gagepage/Pgstory.php

The result of a cut-off of blood supply to a part of the brain is called a **stroke**, or **cerebrovascular accident** (**CVA**). Strokes are caused by deposits to the brain's arteries (**atherosclerosis**), hardening of the arteries (**arteriosclerosis**), clotting in the arteries (**thrombosis**), a clot from somewhere else carried to the brain (**embolism**), arteries bulging out (**aneurysm**), or by arteries bursting (**hemorrhage**).

Beginning in the 1930s, Egas Moniz began performing a type of psychosurgery known as a **lobotomy** or a **frontal lobotomy**. Lobotomies are a type of intentional brain injury. Prior research on dogs and chimpanzees had indicated that the surgical excision (**ablation**) of portions of the cerebral cortex calmed animals. Moniz thought the procedure might be effective in humans with severe mental illness. Moniz surgically cut the nerve fibers connecting a portion of the frontal lobe to the thalamus. No brain matter was removed; the connections were simply cut. Moniz reported that his patients became less agitated and paranoid.

Later, Walter Freeman began performing routine **trans-orbital lobotomies** on children and adults with depression, mania, and schizophrenia. Freeman personally performed over 3,400 lobotomies and taught the procedure in over 50 psychiatric hospitals. Between 1939 and 1951 over 18,000 lobotomies were performed in the United State alone. Freeman eventually performed quick "ice pick" lobotomies by driving an ice pick into the brain through the eye socket with a hammer. He rotated the ice pick to severe the fibers connecting the prefrontal cortex to the rest of the brain. His procedure was so fast that eventually Freeman performed outpatient lobotomies using local anesthesia in an "assembly line" fashion. Though Moniz won a Nobel Prize for his work, lobotomies were misused and caused serious problems for the people who received them. In some cases, families would submit troublesome relatives to a lobotomy. The procedure had serious and lasting consequences for the patients and there are no reports of any lobotomy patient returning to productive work.

For further study read a History of Lobotomy at
http://www.cerebromente.org.br/n02/historia/lobotomy.htm

The Brain and Behavior: Brain Stimulation

Researchers can use weak electric currents to stimulate specific areas of the brain providing insight into the brain's organization and functioning. Early brain stimulation research applied direct electrical impulses to specific areas of the motor cortex. The stimulation consistently produced specific physical reactions. In the 1940s, Wilder Penfield created a map of the motor cortex identifying the parts that controlled the movement of specific body parts. Penfield's map is called the **homunculus**. Later, Penfield and other researchers used electrical stimulation to trigger emotions, thoughts, auditory hallucinations, (hearing sounds, conversations, music, and songs), visual hallucinations, tastes, smells, and detailed memories (some of which were real and others were hallucinated). In 1954 James Olds and Peter Milne, in their research using rats, discovered a **"pleasure center"** in the brain (**hypothalamus**). People receiving electrical stimulation in the pleasure center reported sensations ranging from mildly to intensely pleasurable. Stimulation of the **amygdala** produced feelings of fear, anxiety, and sometimes, violent behavior. Animals whose amygdala was removed showed no fear.

The Brain and Behavior: Brain Imaging

Brain imaging techniques allow researchers to observe brain structures and functioning. Until about 1970 the main technology for studying brain activity was the **electroencephalograph (EEG)**. The EEG records electrical voltage in the brain through electrodes on the scalp. Researchers can correlate the electrical voltage with mental activity. EEGs show brain activity but not brain structure.

Computer axial tomography (CT scan) involves rotating an x-ray machine around the brain to produce series of pictures of the brain. The combined x-ray images produce a 3-dimensional x-ray of the brain. CT scans show brain structure but not brain activity.

Positron emission tomography (PET scan) produces real-time three-dimensional still pictures showing which areas of the brain are active. PET scans measure positrons emitted as brain cells consume glucose. PET scans show brain structure and activity. PET scans have provided important information about the nature of auditory hallucination in schizophrenics, multiple personalities disorders, and even demon possession.

Magnetic Resonance Imaging (MRI) uses powerful magnetic fields to induce a weak radio frequency signal. MRIs, like PET scans, show brain activity. MRIs can show activity in very small areas of the brain.

Basic Unit of the Nervous System: Nerves

Remember that the human nervous system consists of the central nervous system and the peripheral nervous system. To this point this text has only addressed the central nervous system. Before moving to the peripheral nervous system, this section will cover the basic units of the nervous system common to both the central and the peripheral systems; neurons.

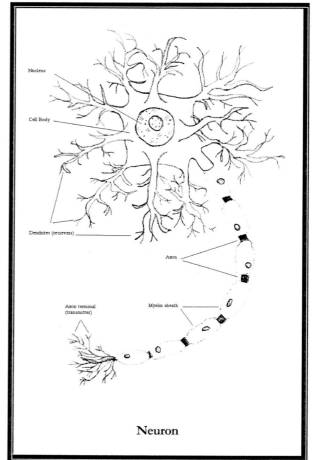

Neuron

Neurons are the cellular building blocks of the nervous system. Our bodies contain billions, if not trillions of neurons. All neurons carry electro-chemical signals. Neurons vary by their size, shape, purpose, and location.

Sensory neurons, as the name implies, carry signals from sense receptors (vision, taste, sound, odor, and touch) toward the central nervous system. Sensory neurons convert environmental stimuli from the environment into electro-chemical signals.

Motor neurons transmit signals from the central nervous system to muscles and glands.

Interneurons exist exclusively in the spinal cord and the brain and make up 90% of all nerve cells in a human. Interneurons are stimulated by signals reaching them from other sensory neurons.

Glia cells, though technically not nerve cells (they do not transmit electro-chemical signals), support neural functioning by digesting dead neurons, producing the myelin sheathing, and providing nutrition to neurons.

Neurons differ from other cells in that they communicate with each other via specialized extensions called **dendrites** and **axons**. The dendrite extends from the cell body much like the branches of a tree (**dendritic tree**). Axons are long and very thin tubes leading away from the cell body. Axons also branch into tree-shaped structures (**axon terminals**).

The classic view of dendrites and axons is that dendrites bring information to the cell body and axons take information away from the cell body. As with the functioning of the brain, researchers have discovered that the process by which neurons transmit signals is far more complex. **Myelin** sheathing surrounds and insulates the axon and works to increase the speed at which signals move along the axon. Neural impulses are electrochemical signals that travel the length of the neuron, generally from the dendrites to the axon. Because the axon branches out, a single neuron may send its signal to thousands of other neurons. Conversely, a single neuron may receive impulses from thousands of neighboring neurons. Introductory psychology courses may describe neurons as simple linear chains when in fact EACH neuron (remember there are billions of them) is connected and coordinated with thousands of other neurons.

Neural impulses travel from one neuron to the next across a **synapse** or **synaptic cleft** (a gap separating neurons). When the impulse reaches the axon of a neuron, molecules (**neurotransmitters**) contained in synaptic vesicles are released into the synaptic cleft. The neurotransmitters move rapidly across the synaptic cleft to receptor sites on the **post-synaptic** (after the synapse) neuron.

Neurotransmitters excite or inhibit the recipient neuron. **Excitatory** neurotransmitters make the post-synaptic neuron more likely to transmit an impulse. **Inhibitory** neurotransmitters make the post-synaptic neuron less likely to transmit a nerve impulse.

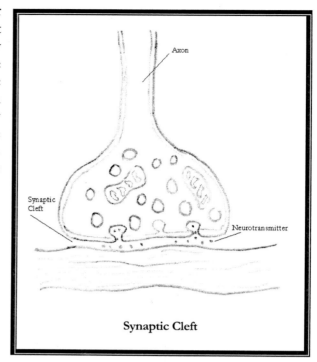

Synaptic Cleft

The Peripheral Nervous System

The **peripheral nervous system (PNS)** consists of those nerves outside of the brain and the spinal cord. The peripheral nervous system is subdivided in the **somatic** and **autonomic** nervous system.

The **somatic (voluntary)** nervous system connects the central nervous system to voluntary skeletal muscles (the muscles used in movement). **Afferent** nerves carry information from the muscles and sense organs to the central nervous system and **efferent** nerves carry information from the CNS to the muscles and sense organs.

The autonomic (involuntary) nervous system controls smooth muscles found in places like the **stomach, intestines, blood vessels, glands, and the bladder.** The autonomic nervous system controls all the automatic functions in the body, including respiration, perspiration, digestion, and heartbeat.

The **autonomic** nervous system is further subdivided into the **sympathetic, parasympathetic,** and **enteric** nervous systems. The sympathetic and parasympathetic systems operate as opposites. The sympathetic system creates an excited state (as in a fight or flight situation). The sympathetic nervous system gets the body ready for emergency action by causing your adrenaline to flow and your heart and breathing rates to increase. The sympathetic system slows digestion, draws blood to the skeletal muscles so the body can act quickly. Where the sympathetic system acts like an accelerator, the parasympathetic systems acts like a brake. The parasympathetic system restores the body to a state of rest and relaxation. It slows your heart and respiration rate, diverts blood flow from the muscles, and restores the digestive process.

The **enteric** nervous system is a network of nerve fibers in the stomach, intestines, pancreas, and gall bladder controlling the digestive process.

For now we see in a mirror, dimly, but then face to face. Now I know in part, but then I shall know just as I also am known (1 Corinthians 13:12).

Sensation and Perception

The processes through which we sense the world around us are very complex. The beauty and wonder of God's creation is for us to enjoy, but for us to enjoy it, it must first pass through our senses. Philosophers and scientists wonder at the marvel of the processes by which we experience and understand the physical world. The processes are well described in most introductory psychology and biology texts. With the exception of the presumption that our senses are the result of evolutionary processes, most texts provide a good overview of the workings of our senses. In this chapter we review the basic physical processes through which sensory organs convert physical energy into nerve impulses.

Sensation is the process through which external physical energy stimulates our sense organs, converts that energy to nerve impulses, and transmits those impulses to the brain. Sensation refers to the experience of the environment through touch, taste, sight, sound, and smell.

Perception is the process through which our brain organizes, interprets,

The famous Rubin goblet illustrates the difference between sensation and perception. The Rubin goblet may be perceived as a goblet or as two faces.

and gives meaning to neural sensations. Sensation and perception are distinct processes that must operate seamlessly for us to experience and interact with the world around us.

Sensation begins with **sensory receptors**; cells designed to respond to particular types of energy. There are four basic types of receptor cells.

- **Photoreceptors** are activated by light.
- **Chemoreceptors** respond to chemicals.
- **Mechanoreceptors** respond to touch or movement.
- **Magnetoreceptors** (not found in humans) respond to magnetic fields.

Sensory receptor cells respond by design to **specific stimuli** but can be made to respond to other types of strong stimulation. For example, a bump on the head (a mechanical stimulus) may stimulate the eye's photoreceptor cells. The result is "seeing stars."

Absolute threshold is the minimum amount of energy necessary to stimulate receptor cells or the point at which a stimulus is noticeable. Early scientific psychological research sought to discover how strong a stimulus had to be before it was noticed. Researchers discovered that the threshold varies from person to person and from time to time for the same person. As a result, the threshold is defined as the point at which a very weak stimulus could be detected 50% of the time.

> The absolute threshold for sight is approximately equivalent to a candle flame thirty miles away on a clear dark night.
>
> For hearing, the threshold is equivalent to the tick of a watch 20 feet away.
>
> For taste, the threshold is equivalent to one teaspoon of sugar in two gallons of water.
>
> For touch, the threshold is equivalent to the wing of a bee falling on your cheek from a distance of 1 centimeter.

Just noticeable difference (JND) refers to receptor cells' ability to detect subtle changes in stimulus strength. How much brighter, louder, warmer, smellier must a stimulus be before we notice the change? The JND is similarly variable and is defined as the smallest change in a stimulus which a person can detect 50% of the time. The JND tends to be a constant expressed as a fraction of the stimulus intensity. For example, if a subject notices the difference between 100 pounds and 102 pounds (2% increase) it does not mean that the subject would notice the difference between 1000 pounds and 1002 pounds. Instead, it would take 20 pounds (2%) before the difference was noticeable. The relationship of sensation to change in stimulus strength is known as **Weber's Law.**

Research has demonstrated that the absolute threshold and JND vary according to several factors. The amount of extraneous stimuli (background noise), the strength of the stimulus, the amount of repeated information in the stimulus, and bias affect signal detection. **Signal detection theory** describes the variables that affect stimulus detection and seeks to explain false positives (noticing a stimulus that is not there) and false negatives (not noticing a stimulus that is there). Researchers have found that they can influence the accuracy at which subjects report noticing a stimulus. By manipulating the consequences of false positives or negatives, researchers found they could increase or decrease the absolute threshold and JND.

Sensory adaptation refers to becoming less sensitive to stimuli that we experience repeatedly or that do not change for an extended period. Why do people who live near highways not notice highway noise and people who live in the country not notice the cricket noise? Sensory adaptation theories suggest answers.

The Visual System

Biologists and psychologists have extensively studied our sense of sight. Sight is our most dominant sense and more of our brain is involved in sight than any other sense. Human sight is a highly sophisticated sensation of reflected electromagnetic radiation (light) from a portion of the electromagnetic spectrum. We experience light as color, brightness, and saturation.

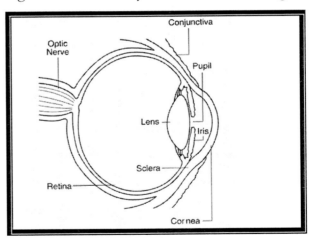

The sensation of sight begins in the eye. The **cornea** refracts (bends and concentrates) the light and creates an upside down image on the back of the eye (the **retina**).

The **iris**, the colored part of the eye located behind the cornea, contains muscles that open or close the **pupil** (the dark center of the iris) to allow in more or less light. Behind the iris, the **lens** focuses the visual image on the back of the eye. The lens is flexible and controlled by a set of muscles that allow it to adjust to focus on objects near or far way.

The retina is rich with millions of specialized light-sensing nerve cells called **rods and cones**. Rods and cones are the receptor cells of the eye (**photoreceptors**). Cones are concentrated in the center of the retina and provide detail and color. Rods provide peripheral vision, detect motion, and help us see in low light. Rods and cones convert light into electrochemical impulses. The optic nerve transmits those impulses to the brain where the image is perceived.

We said earlier that human sight is a highly sophisticated sensation of reflected electromagnetic radiation (light) from a portion of the electromagnetic spectrum. We sense different parts of the electromagnetic spectrum as color. Researchers suggest that we see colors through the interaction of specialized cones and neural pathways. Specialized cones respond to one of three primary colors (red, green, and blue). When we observe other colors (combinations of the primary colors) combinations of cones are stimulated. **Ganglion cells** (specialized nerve cells) receive input from the cones, sort it, and transmit information about color and intensity on to the brain. People who are missing color sensitive cones are said to be **colorblind**.

Other than evolutionary explanations for the biology of vision, there is little conflict between a Christian and a modern psychology worldview in terms of sensation. Perception, however, as the process through which we interpret and give meaning to sensations, is different. Research has indicated that hungry people perceive food-related words faster than those who are not hungry. Research indicates that mood, gender, age, personality, peer influence, experience, values, and religious beliefs affect how we perceive visual sensations. Many theories suggest ways that our brains interpret and give meaning to visual sensations. A Christian view of perception must allow for a spiritual influence on what we see.

The Auditory System

The eye senses electromagnetic radiation (light). The ear senses pressure waves in the air. Sound is the sensation of pressure changes in a medium (usually the air).

> **If a spaceship blew up in space, it would make no sound.**

Sound waves have amplitude and frequency. **Amplitude** describes the wave height (the amount of pressure change) and is a function of the loudness of a sound. **Frequency** describes the number of waves per second and is a function of the pitch of a sound.

The funnel-shaped **auricle** (outer ear) gathers sound pressure waves and directs them down the **auditory canal** to the **eardrum** (**tympanic membrane**). The auricle, auditory canal, and tympanic membrane make up the **outer ear**. The eardrum is a thin, skin-like stretched membrane, much like the skin of a drum. When the sound waves hit the eardrum, it vibrates. Those vibrations pass to a series of small bones (**ossicles**) in the **middle ear**. The ossicles consist of the **hammer (malleus), anvil (incus),** and **stirrup (stapes).** The ossicles are the smallest bones in your body and work to magnify the eardrum's vibrations and to transmit them to the inner ear.

> The Eustachian tube runs from the middle ear to your throat and serves to keep the outside air pressure the same as the middle ear to allow the eardrum to vibrate freely. The Eustachian tube is closed until you swallow or yawn when it opens briefly to equalize air pressure. When you blow your nose too hard, the pain is from too much pressure in the middle ear

The magnified vibrations enter the inner ear at the **oval window**. In the **cochlea** (a hard, snail-shaped, fluid-filled structure) mechanical energy is converted into electrical impulses. As the fluid inside the cochlea moves, electrical impulses in the hair-like **cilia** stimulate nerve impulses that travel along the auditory nerve to structures in the brainstem for further processing. The cilia are a type of **mechanoreceptor.**

For further information watch a slideshow on the ear from the Mayo Clinic at:

http://www.mayoclinic.com/health/ear-infections/EI00027&slide=1

The Olfactory System

At the roof of your nasal cavity is a layer of mucous (**nasal mucosa**) containing the **olfactory epithelium**. The olfactory epithelium holds the **olfactory receptors** (a type of chemoreceptor). The olfactory receptor cells have cilia on one end and an axon on the other. The cilia are specialized to respond to particular chemicals. The axon of the receptors feed directly into the **olfactory bulb**. From the olfactory bulb, signals travel to other parts of the brain including parts involved with memory and emotion (which is why certain smells can bring back memories and the feelings associated with those memories).

The Gustatory System (Taste)

What we experience as taste is actually more about smell than taste. Research suggests that as much as 75% of what we experience as taste actually comes from our sense of smell. Taste begins with taste receptor cells **(gustatory cells)** clustered primarily in **taste buds** on the tongue. Each taste bud is open to the surface of the tongue allowing molecules to reach the receptor cells.

Taste receptor cells are specialized and respond best to a single taste. Taste receptor cells respond to sweet, saline (salt), bitter, and sour. Some researchers suggests we have receptor cells that respond to a fifth taste; glutamate.

Nerve cells in the tongue transmit impulses from the gustatory cells to the brain.

> The small bumps you see on your tongue are not your taste buds. The bumps are called papillae. Your taste buds are inside the papillae.

> Generally, different parts of the tongue taste different flavors, but taste maps like this are over-simplifications.
>
>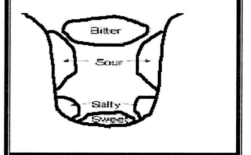

The Cutaneous System (Touch)

The skin is our largest sense organ. Our sense of touch is extremely complex and involves several types of receptor cells. Our sense of touch is part of a larger system that includes our ability to sense both external and internal stimuli. Specialized receptor cells respond to pressure (shape, softness, texture, and vibration), pain (also itches and tickles), temperature, body position, and body movement. Other receptors respond to internal stimuli to provide information from inside the body (i.e. stomach aches and muscle pain). Receptor cells are unevenly distributed. Your fingertips are packed with receptors making them very sensitive.

> Receptors wrapped around hair follicles allow you to feel slight movement in a single hair (try it).

The Kinesthetic System (Movement)

Our **kinesthetic sense** informs us about the position and movement of parts of the body. Without this sense, we could not control voluntary movements (like walking). Our kinesthetic sense allows you to know where your foot is relative to the rest of your body (even when your eyes are closed). The kinesthetic sense plays a big part in allowing you to stumble, but not fall.

Our sense of balance (**equilibrium**) informs us about the position of our body relative to gravity and movement. Fluid-filled organs in the inner ear are oriented along three different planes. Head movement along one of those planes causes the fluid to move, which in turn, is detected and converted to neural impulses. A similar system detects acceleration and deceleration.

> When visual signals are inconsistent with our sense of equilibrium we get motion sickness On a long trip (especially when we're reading in the car), one system tells us that we are moving (the eyes bouncing around the page) but the kinesthetic system senses we are sitting still.

Extrasensory Perception (ESP) and Paranormal Psychology

Ask most people to name the five senses and they will answer with taste, touch, sight, smell, and hearing. They are right, in a sense (pun intended). But you just learned that we have a kinesthetic sense. Humans also can sense infrared radiation and have a limited sensitivity to magnetic fields. These senses, however, have natural explanations. Normal physical processes can explain them and they can be studied in replicable experiments. **Extrasensory perception (ESP)**, however, is said to be the sensation of energy that cannot be measured or studied in replicable experiments. People who have extrasensory perception are said to be **psychic**. The study of ESP is part of parapsychology. **Parapsychology** is the study of paranormal psychological phenomena. Paranormal refers to any phenomena that is not replicable, "physically" impossible, not explainable by natural processes, or beyond the range of normal experience.

Parapsychologist research phenomena like:

- Extra-sensory perception.
- Psychokinetics or moving or affecting physical objects by non-physical methods (mind over matter).

- Survival of consciousness after death, near death experiences, and out-of-body experiences.
- Mental telepathy (the sending and receiving of thought through brain waves).
- Clairvoyance or the ability to see or predict the future.
- Ghosts, mediums, spirit communication, and automatic writing.

A naturalist worldview leads most psychologists to dismiss ESP and parapsychology. Most Christians also dismiss ESP and parapsychology, but for different reasons. Modern psychology dismisses parapsychology because modern psychology denies the existence of the supernatural, but a Christian worldview acknowledges that there is a natural and a supernatural world. A Christian worldview believes that the spiritual can affect the physical world (Matthew 17:20), that our souls do survive after death (John 3:16), and that we can receive messages through "extra sensory" means (Ephesians 1:18). A Christian worldview distinguishes between good spiritual forces (of God) and bad spiritual forces (of the Devil) (Ephesians 6:12). Though parapsychologists generally attribute spiritual power to some benign universal consciousness or power, the Christian must remember that there is no middle ground and should approach parapsychology with the most extreme caution.

Chapter

9

The human brain is a most unusual instrument of elegant and as yet unknown capacity. - Stuart Seaton

Learning

How do animals learn? How do humans learn? Is there a difference between human learning and animal learning? What does the Bible have to say about human learning? Is there a spiritual dimension to learning? Can psychological theories inform a Christian view of human learning? How do the various learning theories fit with a Christian worldview? These are some of the questions facing Christian students as they study the psychology of learning.

In Section 1 you learned that one's worldview (view of God, Mankind, knowledge, right and wrong, and the causes of and cures for mental suffering) directs psychological theory and research. In the introduction to Section II you learned that worldview assumptions led to 6 perspectives on the study of psychology (biological, behavioral, cognitive, psychoanalytic, humanistic, and spiritual). As you might expect, those same worldview assumptions led to different perspectives and theories of learning.

There are at least 53 theories of human learning (see side bar below). Each of the theories takes a biological, behavioral, cognitive, psychoanalytic, humanistic, or combination approach to learning. As you might expect, none are grounded in, or adequately address, the spiritual approach. The author is unaware of any introductory psychology text that addresses the working of the Holy Spirit (Pneumatology) in learning. Our ability to learn is complex and reflects our nature as compound beings, both physical and spiritual. Introductory psychology courses generally emphasize human learning as a complex variation of animal learning. This text suggests that no single approach to or theory of learning is sufficient to explain how we learn. This text suggests that the fullest possible understanding of human learning requires several perspectives, including the spiritual.

The capacity to learn is basic to our lives and involves much more than learning a skill or an academic subject. We must learn to walk and talk, to trust and believe, and to behave according to God's and society's rules. Introductory psychology texts generally define learning as a process leading to relatively permanent (lasting) change in behavior that occurs as a result of prior training, experience, or study. How we learn has been a topic of great interest throughout history and to psychologists since the beginning of modern scientific psychology.

This chapter focuses exclusively on the behavioral perspective on learning (behaviorism). The emphasis on behaviorism is a reflection of the content in most introductory psychology and not a reflection of the merit of that perspective relative to other approaches. The psychology of learning is typically a stand-alone upper-level psychology course.

As with each psychology topic (personality, motivation, cognition, emotions, abnormal psychology, etc.), modern psychology's approach to human learning shifted from a philosophical endeavor to an empirical science and incorporated evolutionary assumptions. It is important that the Christian studying the psychology of learning remember to think about underlying worldview assumptions. It is likewise important that we not pridefully deny the material aspect of our humanity and fail to recognize that we can learn about human learning through animal research. It is important to remember that Christians who reject any knowledge about Mankind derived from study of animals make the same error as psychologists who ignore our God-likeness.

---

53 Theories of Learning

ACT, Adult Learning, Algo-Heuristic , Andragogy, Anchored Instruction, Aptitude-Treatment Interaction, Attribution , Cognitive Dissonance , Cognitive Flexibility , Cognitive Load , Component Display , Conditions of Learning, Connectionism, Constructivist , Contiguity , Conversation , Criterion Referenced Instruction, Double Loop Learning, Drive Reduction , Dual Coding, Elaboration , Experiential Learning, Functional Context , Genetic Epistemology, Gestalt , GOMS, GPS, Information Pickup , Information Processing , Lateral Thinking, Levels of Processing, Mathematical Learning , Mathematical Problem Solving, Minimalism, Model Centered Instruction and Design Layering, Modes of Learning, Multiple Intelligences, Operant Conditioning, Originality, Phenomenonography, Repair , Script , Sign , Situated Learning, Soar, Social Development, Social Learning , Stimulus Sampling , Structural Learning ,Structure of Intellect, Subsumption , Symbol Systems, and Triarchic

---

Learning: Classical Conditioning

Darwinian evolution suggests a continuity of species. Complex organisms are thought to share common ancestry with simple organism. Complex anatomical physical structures and processes are thought to share common ancestry with simple anatomical structures and processes. Early modern psychologists extended evolutionary principles to learning and developed theories that describe human learning as more sophisticated, but not essentially different from animal learning. Those theories began to take shape following the discoveries of Ivan Pavlov.

While doing researching on digestion in dogs, Russian physiologist **Ivan Pavlov** observed an interesting phenomenon. Pavlov's digestion research involved measuring the dogs' secretion of stomach acid and saliva.

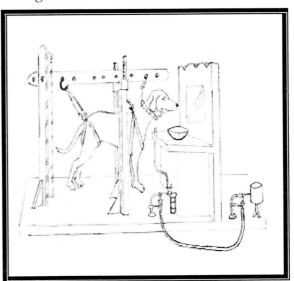

He constructed an apparatus to collect and measure the secretion of saliva. In his digestion research, Pavlov put meat powder in the dog's mouth and measured the amount of saliva excreted. He noticed that after a while, the dogs anticipated the food and began salivating before the powder was put in the mouth. He observed that the dog began salivating at the sight of the food, when the researcher who fed the dogs entered the room, or at the sound of the bell signaling the research assistant to bring the food. Pavlov eventually abandoned his research on digestion and began a long series of experiments to explain the process by which the dogs **learned** non-natural responses to stimuli.

Pavlov prepared the dogs for experimentation by performing a minor operation to expose part of the salivary gland. A valve inserted into the gland collected saliva. The dog was put in a harness behind a one-way glass. Pavlov delivered the meat powder by remote control. After the dog became accustomed to the harness, Pavlov turned on a light. The dog's natural reflexes did not cause it to salivate when the light turned on. When, after a few seconds, Pavlov delivered the meat powder, the dog salivated. After a several trails in which the light was always followed by meat powder, the dog begins to salivate when the light turned on, even if food did not follow. Pavlov's discovery, which he called **signalization**, came to be known as **Classical Conditioning**. Pavlov discovered that when a signal is paired with a natural reflex-producing stimulus, the signal alone begins to activate a learned response similar to the natural reflex. The process of leaning the response is known as **acquisition**.

> **Assignment 9.1**
>
> **Design an experiment using the principles of classical conditioning to determine if dogs can tell the difference between red and green light.**

The key components of classical conditioning are:

- A **reflex.** Classical conditioning always starts with a **reflex.** Reflexes are not learned. Dogs reflexively salivate when given meat powder.

- The **unconditioned stimulus (UCS).** The UCS is a stimulus that naturally elicits a biological reflex. Meat is an unconditioned stimulus for a dog.

> **Assignment 9.2**
>
> **In your own words, explain a NS, UCS, CS, UCR, and CR.**
>
> **In your own words, explain how a neutral stimulus becomes conditioned stimulus.**

- The **unconditioned response (UCR).** The UCR is a natural response to a stimulus. Salivation is a dog's unconditioned response to meat.

- A **neutral stimulus (NS).** The neutral stimulus does not elicit a reflexive response. The sound of a metronome (or a bell or light) is a neutral stimulus to a dog.

- A **conditioned stimulus (CS).** The CS is a previously neutral stimulus that, after being associated with the unconditioned stimulus, eventually elicits a conditioned response.

- A **conditioned response (CR).** The conditioned response is the learned response to the previously neutral stimulus. The unconditioned response and conditioned response are similar, but not identical. The conditioned and unconditioned responses have different causes and they occur and at different strengths. The conditioned response to a conditioned stimulus is generally weaker than the unconditioned response to an unconditioned stimulus. A dog does not drool as much to the sound as if to for real food.

By repeatedly pairing the light or sound (neutral stimulus) with the meat powder (UCS), the light or sound alone began to elicit a response. The dogs learned to associate the conditioned stimulus (CS) with the unconditioned stimulus (UCS). The sound (neutral stimulus) became a conditioned stimulus (CS). The learned response is known as a conditioned response (CR).

The reverse of acquisition is **extinction**. A conditioned response (salivation) stops when the conditioned stimulus (sound) is repeatedly **not** paired with the unconditioned stimulus (meat). In the case of Pavlov's dog, when the sound no longer signaled the arrival of food, the dog eventually stopped salivating in response to the sound. Extinction eliminates the predictive relationship between the signal and the reflex. **Spontaneous recovery** refers to the reappearance of an extinguished conditioned response when the conditioned stimulus returns after a period of absence.

> **Classical conditioning 101**
>
> **Meat causes dogs to drool.**
>
> **Pair meat with sound and the dog still drools.**
>
> **Eventually the sound alone causes the dog to drool.**

> *Desensitization* is a therapeutic technique that applies the principles of extinction to people. If you were, as a result of being bitten by a dog as a child, frightened of dogs, repeated exposure to dogs that did not bite you might *desensitize* you and eliminate your fear of dogs (extinguish the conditioned response).

Generalization refers, as you might guess, to the same conditioned response to similar but not identical stimuli. After using a particular tone to condition his dogs, Pavlov varied the tones and measured the extent to which the different tones stimulated a response. He found that the degree to which the training and testing tones were similar was related to the amount of salivation. The opposite of generalization is **discrimination**. Discrimination occurs when one stimulus triggers a conditional response but another does not. In the case of Pavlov's dog, the dog that salivated (CR) to a metronome (CS) but did not salivate to a violin discriminated between stimuli.

Higher-order conditioning refers to pairing an unconditioned stimulus with a conditioned stimulus. Consider the dog conditioned to salivate to a sound. If a light were paired with the sound, eventually the dog would begin to salivate at the sight of the light alone even though the light had not been paired directly with the food. The light is a higher-order conditioned stimulus.

John B. Watson, an American who studied Pavlov's work, also conducted classical conditioning research. Watson connected subjects' fingertips to wiring allowing him to administer mild electric shocks. Watson rang a bell and then administered a shock to the subjects' fingertips. The electricity caused the subject to involuntarily move his/her finger. After only a few pairings, the subject would move his/her finger whenever the bell rang, even if it was not followed by a shock.

Learning: Operant Conditioning

The principles of classical conditioning explain much about animal learning. It seems intuitively important that animals be able to associate a stimulus with a biologically significant event. But for much behavior there is no reflex-producing triggering stimulus. Remember that early psychology's worldview emphasized observable behavior. They sought reducible mechanistic explanations for all behavior. Classical conditioning was insufficient to explain complex behaviors and linking all behaviors back to reflex producing stimuli was very cumbersome. **Edward L. Thorndike** suggested that learning depended less on reflexes and more on feedback from (consequences of) behavior.

Thorndike used cats and "puzzle boxes" to study learning. He placed cats in boxes that had only one way out. To escape, the cat had to open the box door by pressing a specific area of the box. In the course of the cat's seemingly random efforts to escape, it accidentally pressed the right spot and opened the door. On subsequent attempts the cat tried to repeat what it had done before. After repeated trials, the cat could escape quickly and efficiently. Thorndike suggested a "**Law of Effect**" to describe the cat's behavior. The law of effect states that any behavior that has good consequences will tend to be repeated and any behavior that has bad consequences will tend to be avoided. The key distinction between classical conditioning (Pavlov) and Thorndike's work was the reward. The puzzle box rewarded the cat's desired responses. In classical conditioning, animals anticipated a stimulus.

Operant Conditioning: B. F. Skinner

In the 1930s, **B. F. Skinner**, the "father of operant conditioning," more fully developed and extended the theory of operant conditioning. Skinner believed that animals (and humans) learn to "operate" (hence the term "operant") on the environment to gain rewards and avoid negative consequences. Skinner did not disagree with Pavlov. He understood that the environment provides cues that affect behavior but he was more interested in the effect of consequences on behavior. He believed that animals and human learn that rewards, punishments, and negative consequences are contingent on behavior.

Pavlov is remembered for his salivating dogs. Skinner is known for his animal boxes (**Skinner box**). A Skinner box is a small box in which an animal (usually a rat) can automatically get a food reward for a certain response. The box contains equipment that records the number of responses the animal makes. A typical Skinner box contains a food pellet dispenser (magazine), a response lever, a light or buzzer, and

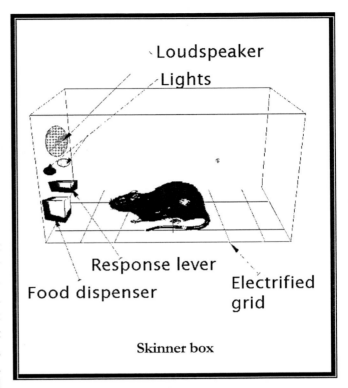

Skinner box

the capacity to administer an electric shock through the floor grid. Operant conditioning begins with magazine training. The researcher releases a food pellet into the magazine, the hungry rat smells it, finds it, and eats it. The process is repeated until the rat "learns" the location of food and "associates" the clinking sound of a pellet dropping into the magazine with food. The rat is conditioned to respond to the sound of a pellet dropping into the magazine. A **response** (running to the food magazine) to a stimulus (the sound of the pellet) is **reinforced** (with food).

Next the rat's behavior is "shaped." **Shaping** describes reinforcing successive approximations of the desired behavior. The research wants the rat to press the lever (the **target behavior**). The researcher shapes the rat's behavior by first delivering a food pellet when the rat faces the lever and then when the rat is near the lever. The rat learns and soon stays near the lever. If, by chance, the rat should touch or press the lever, the researcher delivers a pellet. Eventually the rat must touch and then press the lever before it receives a pellet. Before long the rat learns to press the lever for food.

Introductory psychology courses generally devote considerable time to the principles of operant conditioning. A student who memorizes the terminology will be ahead of the game.

- **Reinforcement:** A consequence of a behavior that increases the likelihood that a response will occur.
- **Positive Reinforcement:** A consequence of behavior that is usually pleasant (i.e. food, money, praise) and increases the likelihood of a response
- **Primary Reinforcer:** A consequence of behavior that is inherently reinforcing (i.e. food and water).
- **Secondary Reinforcer:** A consequence of behavior that is reinforcing through association with a primary reinforcer (i.e. money).
- **Negative reinforcement:** A consequence of behavior in which a negative stimulus is removed. Remember that all reinforcement increases the likelihood of a response. Negative reinforcement increases the likelihood of a response by removing an unpleasant stimulus. Generally, positive reinforcement introduces a pleasant consequence and negative reinforcement removes a negative consequence.
- **Punishment:** A consequence of a behavior that decreases the likelihood that a response will occur.
- **Positive punishment:** A consequence of behavior that is usually unpleasant (i.e. pain) and decreases the likelihood of a response.
- **Negative punishment** (sometimes known as "time-out"): A consequence of behavior in which a positive stimulus is removed. Remember that all punishment decreases the likelihood of a response. Negative punishment decreases the likelihood of a response by removing a pleasant stimulus. Generally, positive punishment introduces an unpleasant consequence and negative punishment removes a pleasant stimulus.
- **Primary punisher:** A consequence of behavior that is inherently unpleasant.
- **Secondary punisher:** A consequence of behavior that is unpleasant through association with a primary punisher.
- **Reinforcement schedule:** The frequency or pattern of reinforcement. A behavior does not have to be reinforced every time it occurs. Reinforcement schedules can be continuous or intermittent.
- **Continuous reinforcement schedule:** The desired behavior is reinforced every time it occurs.
- **Intermittent reinforcement schedule:** The desired behavior is reinforced some of the time. There are two categories of

intermittent reinforcement schedules; ratio and interval. There are four types of intermittent reinforcement schedules; fixed ratio, variable ratio, fixed interval, and variable interval.

- **Fixed ratio reinforcement schedule:** Reinforcement happens after a fixed number of responses. For example, the rat receives a food pellet after every fifth response. The passage of time does not make reinforcement more likely.

- **Fixed interval reinforcement schedule:** Reinforcement happens after a fixed amount of time. For example, the rat receives a food pellet for a response every two minutes.

- **Variable ratio reinforcement schedule:** Reinforcement happens after a number of responses. The passage of time does not make reinforcement more likely. In the case of the Skinner box, the rat receives a food pellet after an average of five responses.

- **Variable interval reinforcement schedule:** Reinforcement happens after a variable period of time. In the case of the Skinner box, the rat receives a food pellet for a response after an average of two minutes.

- **Extinction:** The gradual disappearance of a response when reinforcement ceases.

- **Shaping:** Shaping guides behavior toward the desired response by reinforcing successively approximations of desired behavior. In the case of the Skinner box, the rat receives reinforcement for looking at the bar, then for sniffing the bar, touching the bar, and then for pressing the bar.

- **Behavioral Chaining:** Chaining teaches complex behaviors by reinforcing simpler behaviors in a sequence.

> **Different reinforcement schedules produce different rates of responses. Variable schedules produce steady rates of response because reinforcement is less predictable. Slot machines are programmed to payoff on a variable ratio schedule.**
>
> **In fixed reinforcement schedules, responses start slowly and increase just before the reinforcement occurs. Variable reinforcement schedules are more resistant to extinction.**

Classical conditioning does not produce new behavior, but it can explain some learning. Operant conditioning can however, produce and explain some (if not all) very complex behaviors in animals. Rats can learn to press a bar for food only when a green light is on. Pigeons can learn to play a piano and chimpanzees can learn to use a computer. Principles of conditioning can teach children to sit still in a classroom, eat their vegetables, and to look both ways before crossing a street. In adults the principles have helped people overcome anxiety, substance abuse, and irrational fears.

Assignment 9.3

Read *Behavioral Psychology in the Sunday School Classroom* at

www.asa3.org/asa/PSCF/1982/JASA12-82Ratcliff.html

Some behaviorists believe that classical and operant conditioning can explain all behavior (including **all** human behavior). In Section I this text described behaviorism's worldview assumptions. Those worldview assumptions extend to classical and operant conditioning. Questions about determinism, reductionism, and responsibility contribute to vigorous denunciations by many in Christendom of the application of behavioral approaches to human leaning. As a model of Mankind, behaviorism is shallow. As an explanation of all human behavior, behaviorism is woefully insufficient. As a partial model explaining some of the ways in which humans learn, behaviorism has merit.

Assignment 9.4

1. Define Operant Conditioning

4. Understand: Reinforcement, positive reinforcement, negative reinforcement, punishment, extinction, and reinforcement schedules.

5. Explain in your own words the similarities and differences between punishment and negative reinforcement. (Good research resources at http://allpsych.com/psychology101/learning.html and http://tip.psychology.org/skinner.html)

6. Read B.F. Skinner's "Superstition in the Pigeon" accessible at http://academic.udayton.edu/gregelvers/hop/index.asp?m=3&a=83&key=137

Chapter 10

The moment we try to fix our attention upon consciousness and to see what, distinctly, it is, it seems to vanish. George Edward Moore

In section I, this text explained that as the study of psychology approaches the core issues of the nature of Mankind, the greater the potential for conflict with a Christian worldview. As psychology's subject matter approaches the core of Biblical anthropology, the greater the risk of accepting theories grounded in anti-Christian worldviews. The nature of consciousness is near to the core of what it means to be human and the heart of the Bible's message.

Pre-modern and very early modern psychology focused extensively on the nature of consciousness. As early modern psychologists established the discipline as a natural science, it moved away from reliance on introspection, self-reports, and the examination of mental processes. The focus on observable behavior left concepts like consciousness unexamined. In the 1950s and 60s, the rise of cognitive and humanistic psychology produced a renewed interest in the study of consciousness. The renewed interest did not however, include a spiritual perspective on the nature of consciousness. The Christian studying psychology must not accept definitions of consciousness that leave God out of the picture.

Consciousness

What is consciousness? What does it mean to be conscious? Are animals conscious? If so, how does human consciousness differ from animal consciousness? Is consciousness subject to scientific investigation? If so, what are the brain mechanisms of consciousness? New technologies, particularly brain scanning technology, have provided new insight into conscious and unconscious mental processes. But many questions remain.

Consciousness is difficult to define and there is no widely accepted definition. It has been defined as:

- The awareness one has of one's self and of the environment.
- The capacity to be explicitly aware of ourselves and to make explicit free-well decisions.
- The ability to establish meaningful relationships.
- The subjective experiencing of a stimulus or mental state.
- The ability to attribute goals (either to oneself or to others).

- The locus for human decision-making.
- The essence of Mankind's God-likeness.

A Christian worldview sees consciousness as the vehicle of our relationships with God and others. Consciousness is a pre-requisite of free will. Free will is a pre-requisite of moral accountability. The principles of free will and moral accountability are central to the Christian worldview. Without moral accountability, sin and salvation are meaningless. Without consciousness, humans are nothing more than very complex animals. Descriptions of humans as nothing more than "rational animals" (without consciousness) clearly diverge from a Christian view of Mankind.

For the Christian studying psychology, the study of consciousness means understanding our God-given self-awareness in the context of the complexity of our underlying nervous system. The student must balance the discoveries made in neuroscience with the supernatural component our consciousness. The student must recognize that because our experience of consciousness is inherently subjective, consciousness, whatever it is, is not subject to the usual objective methods of natural science.

Modern psychology, as you might guess, seeks descriptions and explanations of consciousness in terms of evolutionary processes. Not only does modern psychology struggle to define consciousness, it struggles to describe a theory of how it evolved. To explain consciousness in terms of evolution, one must acknowledge that it exists, describe its structure and process in the nervous system, and describe how it enhanced survival and reproduction. It appears to the author that not only does the risk to the Christian student increase as psychology nears the heart of what it means to be human, so do the lengths to which theorists will go to explain away the supernatural. Many scientists suggest that brain structures and processes can explain consciousness. They await the development of new technologies to enable them to "find" the mechanics of consciousness, confident that it is just another reducible component of Mankind, not qualitatively different than the animals.

> **For further study:**
>
> **Dr. Giulio Tononi proposes a "dynamic core" of neurons that work in concert in human consciousness. Others suggest quantum physics hold the answers to the mystery of consciousness. Read an article on Dr. Tononi's work at**
> www.neuropsychiatryreviews.com/oct02/npr_oct02_consciousness.html

States of Consciousness

The study of consciousness is made more difficult by the fact that it is not a single constant mental state. Dreams, hypnosis, meditation, hallucinations, and ecstasy are variations of consciousness. Psychoactive drugs alter consciousness, as do extremes of heat, fatigue, exhaustion, dehydration, and malnutrition. Different patterns of brain waves are associated with different states of consciousness. Brain waves describe patterns of electrical activity in the brain. We begin our discussion of states of consciousness with an examination of sleep.

Sleep

Humans spend about one-third of their lives asleep. Sleep is more than a simple state of unconsciousness. While we sleep our brains continue to work. Like there are several states of waking consciousness, sleep comprises several states or stages. We dream, we talk, and some walk in their sleep. Mothers waken easily at the sound of their baby and some people "program" themselves to wake at the same time every day.

There was little research into sleep until the 1950s and the discovery that our eyes move while we sleep. The discovery of **rapid eye movements (REM)** began a time of intensive research into the nature of sleep. REM sleep refers to a distinctive sleep stage during which we dream, breathing fluctuates, heart rates go up and down, traces of muscle activity appear across the body, and our eyes move rapidly back and forth (up to 8 times each second). During REM sleep, our brain wave activity is very similar to brain activity when we are awake, alert, and thinking.

In one night's sleep, we pass through five stages. We move through the stages (stages 1-4 and REM) three or four times each night. Some texts refer the "awake but ready for sleep" state as stage 0. Patterns of brain waves vary according to sleep stage. There are four main types of brain waves: alpha, beta, theta, and delta. **Beta waves** are characteristic of alertness, thought, and concentration (an engaged mind). Beta waves have low amplitude (15 to 40 cycles per second.) When we are

An electroencephalogram (EEG) measures and records the electrical brain activity of your brain.

An electromyograph (EMG) records muscle activity.

An electrooculograph (EOG) records eye movements.

An electrocardiograph (EKG) records the activity of the heart.

awake but sleepy with our eyes closed (stage 0), EEGs show mostly alpha waves. **Alpha waves** are slower (9 to 14 cycles per second) and higher in amplitude. Alpha waves indicate rest, decreased attention to the environment, and the beginning of sleep. In stage 1 sleep the EEG shows mostly theta waves. **Theta waves** have even greater amplitude and slower frequency (5 to 8 cycles per second). In stage 1 sleep, the heart and breathing rates drop, body temperature drops, and muscles relax. Alpha waves and our attention to the environment disappear. During stage 1 sleep, we may experience odd or bizarre mental images.

After a few minutes of stage 1 sleep, people move into about twenty minutes of stage 2 sleep. Stage 2 is characterized by short bursts of distinctive EEG patterns called sleep spindles and K-complex. A **K-complex** is a brief burst of voltage that may occur in response to sound. **Sleep spindles** are short bursts of brain activity that may represent the brain's effort to keep us relaxed. Tossing and turning often accompanies stage 1 and 2 sleep.

> **The Hypnagogic State**
> During the transition from wakefulness to sleep, some people experience visual or auditory hallucinations or a falling sensation. Some may interpret the experience as ESP, ghosts, or out-of-body experiences.
>
> **Sleep jerk**
>
> About 70% of people report occasionally, just after falling asleep, waking suddenly to a falling sensation and a strong muscle twitch. Sleep jerks are more accurately known as a hypnagogic myoclonic twitch.

In stages 3 and 4 brain waves slow even more and we pass into deep sleep. **Delta waves**, characteristic of stages 3 and 4, have the greatest amplitude and slowest frequency (1.5 to 4 cycles per second). People in stage 3 sleep have slow breathing and heart rates, very relaxed muscles, and are difficult to rouse. In stage 4, body functions decline to the deepest state of rest, we move little, and the sleeper is virtually oblivious to the environment. Someone awakened from stage 4 sleep will be groggy, disoriented, and confused.

As noted earlier, we move through the sleep stages three or four times each night. We do not however, move from stage 1 to 4 to REM sleep and then start over again with stage 1. For the

> **Do you know when you fall asleep?**
>
> The average teenager takes 15 minutes to fall asleep. Many fall asleep in fewer than 6 minutes. The average teenager thinks that it takes more than 30 minutes to fall asleep.

first one or two cycles of sleep stages we do progress from stage 1 to stage 4 and then to REM sleep. In later cycles we move through the cycles in reverse. Some people get all the deep sleep they need during the first few cycles and spend the rest of the night in lighter sleep. Sleep patterns, especially following days of intense physical activity are characterized by more stage 4 and 5 sleep.

The "average" adult sleeps about 7 hours each night, but our need for sleep decreases until adulthood after which it remains stable. Though the *average* adult needs about 7 hours of sleep each night, some people function with 4 or 5 hours each night and others need 10 or 11 hours. As a newborn, you probably slept about 18 hours each day. As a baby, about half of your sleep was REM sleep.

Sleep deprivation refers to the lack of adequate sleep. **REM deprivation** refers to the lack of adequate REM sleep. Brief periods of sleep deprivation (pulling an all-nighter to study for a test) have few if any physical consequences. After short periods of sleep deprivation our bodies compensate with more REM sleep. Extreme sleep deprivation however, can have serious effects on mental and physical health. Chronic sleep deprivation sleep impairs thinking, concentration, memory, the ability to manage stress, and the ability to fight infection. Laboratory animals deprived of sleep die within three weeks. It is very difficult for humans to voluntarily go without sleep for more than 48 hours. After long periods without sleep, people lose motor coordination, have difficulty speaking, and may experience auditory and visual hallucinations.

> The world record for the longest period without sleep is 11 days. In 1965 Randy Gardner stayed awake 11 days without using stimulants. After four days without sleep, Gardner began hallucinating and believed he was actually a famous football player.

Though the amount of sleep we need levels off after childhood and remains stable, our sleep patterns change and we are more likely to experience sleep difficulties as we age. Around middle age, we begin spending less time in stage 3 and 4 sleep. As a result of sleeping less soundly, we wake more easily. Age-related hormonal and physical changes affect the quality our sleep.

Our pattern of sleep is part of a set of daily physiological cycles (rhythms). A **circadian rhythm** is a 24-hour physiological cycle. The word circadian comes from the Latin, meaning "around one day." Sleep, body temperature, alertness, blood pressure, elimination, and hormone levels follow circadian rhythms. Circadian rhythms are influenced by environmental cues (i.e. daylight and darkness) but they are not dependent on them. Daily rhythms will synchronize with the environment, but research indicates circadian rhythms continue even without environmental cues; suggesting that the brain has a way to keep track of time. **Jet lag** refers to the fatigue and disorientation air travelers feel after a long flight when environmental cues do not match the circadian rhythm.

Somnambulism or **sleepwalking** is one of a group of sleep disorders in which activities normally done while awake are done while asleep. Sleepwalkers perform tasks (cleaning, walking around, cooking) as though they were wide-awake. The sleepwalker's eyes are generally open, but appear "glassy" or "vacant." Sleepwalkers are not conscious of their actions at a level allowing memories to form, so if the sleepwalker returns to bed before waking, he/she usually does not remember. Research suggests that sleepwalkers are not acting out dreams. Sleepwalking is more common in children and is associated with high levels of stress and anxiety. Because sleepwalkers are in deep stage 3 or 4 sleep, they are difficult to waken and may be disoriented and groggy when awakened. Waking up someplace other than bed may be frightening, so many suggest that it is best to just lead the sleepwalker back to bed.

Somniloquy or **sleep talking** is another normally harmless sleep disorder. It refers to talking out-loud during sleep. Sleep talking may occur during any sleep stage and the speech may be soft or loud, it may be difficult to understand, nonsensical, or perhaps vulgar and offensive. It is unclear if sleep talking is always associated with dreaming but at times it is a verbal expression of dream content. Sleep talking is common and occurs in 50% of young children. Most stop sleep talking by puberty, but about 5% of adults talk in their sleep.

Narcolepsy is a very serious sleep disorder in which people fall asleep suddenly and without warning, while performing ordinary activities. People with narcolepsy experience excessive daytime sleepiness and may go directly into deep sleep. We all experience sleepiness, but someone with narcolepsy falls asleep at inappropriate times. Narcolepsy is particularly dangerous because it is frequently accompanied by a complete loss of voluntary muscle control (**cataplexy).** Researchers believe that narcolepsy is a neurological condition in which the brain does not regulate sleep-wake cycles normally.

Sleep apnea is relatively common sleep disorder (The NIH estimates that 12 million Americans have it) with potentially negative effects on health. The word apnea is from the Greek and means "without breath." During normal sleep, we occasionally stop breathing, but after a few seconds, we begin to breathe again without any disturbance to our sleep. In sleep apnea, however, each time breathing stops (as often as 20 to 30 times each hour), the sufferer briefly wakens to gasp for air. Obviously, waking 20 to 30 times each hour interferes with proper sleep. Though people at any age can have sleep apnea, it is associated with overweight males over 40 years old.

There are two types of apnea: obstructive and central. In **obstructive sleep apnea**, the soft tissue in the throat collapses and closes during sleep. People with obstructive sleep apnea often snore loudly. In **central sleep apnea**, the brain fails to signal the muscles to breathe. Daytime drowsiness (and the accompanying risk for accidents), headaches, irritability, memory problems, weight gain, and increased risk of high blood pressure, heart attack, stroke, and diabetes are possible consequences of untreated sleep apnea.

Sleep paralysis describes the experience of being awake but temporarily unable to move or speak. Sleep paralysis occurs as we are just falling asleep or as we are just becoming fully awake. People suffering from sleep paralysis may report feeling fear and "some sort of presence," but are unable to cry out. The experience usually last a few seconds after which one feels suddenly released.

> **The Hypnopompic State**
>
> During the transition between sleep and wakefulness, some people experience a state of dis-orientation and confusion that may include hallucinations.

REM behavior disorder (RBD) is a sleep disorder that involves acting-out vivid, intense, and sometimes violent dreams. The behaviors include yelling, screaming, hitting, grabbing, punching, kicking, and generally flailing around. There is no known cause for RBD, but it is thought to be related to a malfunction of the area in the brain responsible for inhibiting motion during sleep. Some have suggested that the disorder is associated with neurological degeneration; perhaps Parkinson disease. RBD occurs during REM sleep when the brain is highly active and experiencing vivid images. In a person with RBD, the muscular paralysis that normally occurs during REM sleep is absent. RBD episodes may occur rarely or up to four times each night. RBD is rare (less than 1%). It is usually seen in men of middle age or older but it can appear at any age. Episodes tend to get worse over time.

Dreams

Dreaming is a universal human experience. When we dream, we encounter experiences, sights, sounds, ideas, and emotions. Most dreams are very ordinary. Some are extraordinary.

> During the typical lifespan, six years are spent dreaming.

Most are outside the control of the dreamer. My dreams and yours are not alike in length, content, emotions, or vividness. Research suggests that everybody dreams four or five times a night.

Not all dreams occur during REM sleep. Dreams occur during each sleep stage. During REM sleep (also known as paradoxical sleep), brain wave activity closely resembles that of wakefulness and dreams are generally more vivid. Dreams during non-REM sleep generally contain fragmented thoughts and images and are difficult to remember. Non-REM dreams are less like being in a different world and more like thinking about the day's events. Narrative dreams, weird dreams, and nightmares are characteristic of REM sleep. The content of dreams is similar across all cultures. Research suggests that dreams of falling, being chased, being injured, a loved one being injured, flying, and being nude in public may be universal dreams.

Brains scans strongly suggest that dreaming involves the prefrontal cortex. The pre-frontal cortex (also known as the executive function) is associated with our conscious ability to distinguish, evaluate, plan, and predict.

Meaning of Dreams

What are dreams? What do they mean? How does the experience of dreams fit with a Christian worldview? Is there a Christian view of dreams? If so, how does the Christian view compare to the view of modern psychology. Are dreams simply subconscious mental processes or are they a

> **Assignment 10.1**
>
> **Read Matt. 1:20, 2:12-13, and 27:19.**

means through which God communicates to us? If God chooses to reveal Himself through the imagery of dreams, how do we understand and interpret the imagery?

Mystics of every tradition throughout history valued the meaning of dreams. Modern mystics of every tradition assign value and meaning to dreams. Many see dreams as evidence of a mystical spiritual realm. Popular literature contains countless guides to dream symbols and dream interpretation.

Evolutionary theory suggests that dreams developed as a way to rehearse strategies to survive in a hostile environment. Early humans, as the theory goes, who could dream about surviving a saber-tooth tiger attack were more likely to survive and reproduce than those who did not dream. They suggest that the common "being chased" dream is evidence for the theory.

Some theorize that dreams are the prefrontal cortex's attempt to make sense out of random neural impulses (brain sparks). Some see dreams as mental housekeeping, like a computer hard drive that needs periodic defragmenting. Some theorists believe dreams are how the brain eliminates, strengthens, and re-organizes neural connections.

Freud theorized that dreams provide an unconscious outlet for the violent and sexual urges we suppress while conscious. Freud believed that dreams contained **latent** (hidden) meanings. For example, if a dream included a cigar, Freud believed that the cigar represented a penis and that the latent meaning of the dream was sexual. Many today suggest that dreams serve to cleanse us of emotional arousal or as a way to "deal" with guilt, worry, trauma, or death.

Carl Jung saw dreams as symbolic representations of memories and instincts shared by all people. Eric Fromm saw dreams as unconscious problem solving. Many today see dreams as unconscious expressions of our conscious concerns providing unconscious insight into solving those problems. Some see dreams as cosmic messages from the spirit world. The "meaningful dreams" are thought to provide warning, direction, advice, or inspiration. Others see dreams as evidence of their pantheistic worldview; that Mankind, god, and the universe are "one."

A Christian View of Dreams

The Bible is rich with examples of God speaking through dreams. In the Old Testament, God chose to communicate to select people of Israel through dreams. God continued to communicate through dreams in the New Testament. He may have indicated His intent to communicate though dreams today. The early Church fathers believed dreams were a continuing source of revelation. If God continues to communicate through dreams, how are we to interpret the content?

> **Assignment: 10.2**
>
> **Read Gen. 28:10-15 and Gen. 41:1-33.**

Achieving a Christian view of dreams is made more difficult by the Biblical cautions of false dreams and warnings about lies in the form of dreams. The Bible is clear that the Gospel message is complete. If dreams have no role in further "revelation," do they have a role as a means of "illumination" for the individual dreamer?

> **Assignment 10.3**
>
> **Read Gen. 40:8, Joel 2:28, Deut. 13:1-3, and Jer. 23:25-28.**

If our dream life is part of our God-likeness, if God still speaks through dreams, the Christian student of psychology must, as is the case in most of psychology's content, guard against exclusively naturalistic explanations of dreams. We must not simply dismiss dreams as meaningless unconscious imagery. If we seek meaning in our dreams, we should not accept completely secular interpretations and, as a prelude to this text's discussion of psychotherapies, the Christian student must be cautious and wise when Christian dreamers claim special revelation through dreams or special ability to interpret dreams

James Ryle, a prominent Christian leader, wrote a book published in 1993. In *Hippo in the Garden*, Ryle described a dream in which he saw a man leading a hippopotamus into a garden. Ryle interpreted the dream as a message from God announcing a coming charismatic prophetic movement.

Hypnosis

Hypnosis is an altered, trance-like state of consciousness in which a person is **hyper-suggestible** (easily influenced). Is hypnosis a tool of the occult? Is hypnosis real? Is hypnosis just a highly focused state of attentive concentration? In a hypnotic state, is one more in tune with God's consciousness? Hypnosis is controversial. Hypnosis is interesting. Some suggest that in Genesis 2:21-22, when Adam fell into a deep sleep, God performed the first hypnosis. There are references to hypnotic-like states in ancient Egyptian and Greek literature, but **Franz Anton Mesmer** (not God) is usually credited with the discovery of hypnosis.

Mesmer's techniques, known at the time as **mesmerization**, were focused on healing illness by manipulating **animal magnetism** (mysterious energy fields surrounding living creatures). Using magnets and crude batteries to induce trance-like convulsions, Mesmer believed body fluids were restored to their proper flow. The Marquis de Puysegur, a student of Mesmer, learned that convulsions were not necessary. Puysegur induced trance-like states with words. Healing was often a result of Puysegur's "suggestions."

In the early 19th century, James Braid developed a form of **hypnotic induction** using eye fatigue to induce a hypnotic trance. In Braid's model, the hypnotist held a shiny object slightly above the subject's eye level while suggesting the subject was "getting very, very sleepy" and that their eyelids were "getting very, very, heavy." With a steady gaze on an object above eye level and continuous suggestions (sleep talk), the subject's eyelids did get heavy and they did get sleepy. Using increasingly demanding suggestions, the subject was asked to concentrate on small changes in the body or the environment and told to go to an ever deeper and more relaxed sleep. Once in the altered state, the subject acted, perceived, thought, and felt according to the hypnotist's suggestions. The hypnotized person accepted the instructions of a hypnotist much the way a dreaming person accepts strange events in a dream. This allowed the hypnotist to suggest behaviors or perceptions that otherwise would not occur. Classic examples are taking a bite of an onion but interpreting it as an apple, accepting the suggestion that his/her arm is paralyzed, or not experiencing severe pain. While hypnotized, people will respond to suggestions that they see things that are not there and not see things that are there. Under hypnotic suggestion people will remember long forgotten events, recall events that did not happen, and forget events that really happened (**posthypnotic amnesia**). Under deep hypnosis, suggestions can be issued for later execution (**post-hypnotic suggestion**). Under hypnosis, subjects have gone temporarily deaf, undergone surgery without anesthesia, and have been said to "regress" to a younger age.

Not everyone can be hypnotized and some people are more hypnotizable than others. About 5-10% of people do not respond to hypnosis. Psychologists do not agree about what hypnosis is. They do not agree that hypnosis is an altered state of consciousness. The hypnotic state is not sleep; brain waves do not change as in sleep. Some theorists suggest that hypnosis causes the subject to divide their consciousness into two parts; one part that responds to the outside world and one part that does not. Some suggest that the hypnotized person is faking or playing a role.

Hypnosis: A Christian View?

What is the relationship of a Christian worldview, modern psychology, and hypnosis? In terms of hypnosis, a better question may be "how do Christian worldviews differ?"

Earlier you learned that a Christian worldview and modern psychology interact around 5 main worldview components.

- What do you believe about God?
- What do you believe about nature of Mankind?
- What do you believe about the nature of knowledge?
- What do you believe about the nature of right and wrong?
- What do you believe about the causes of and cures for mental suffering?

Christians disagree with other Christians over whether hypnotism is an acceptable for Christians. Some say that hypnosis is a type of idolatry or the practice of a false religion. They include hypnosis with Zen Buddhism and other Eastern religions. Christian critics of hypnosis compare the hypnotic trance with the yogic trance. They see hypnosis as a religious activity in which one's mind merges with the universal consciousness. If that is what hypnosis is, the Christian is well-advised to avoid it.

Some believe that hypnosis is an occult practice (see Leviticus 19:31) and that hypnosis leaves one open to satanic attack. Hypnotists who claim to be able to contact the dead, to lead us to past or future lives, or to be able divine the future are, according to a Christian worldview, practicing the occult. Some say that in a hypnotic trance we relinquish control of ourselves to the hypnotist or perhaps to Satan. If hypnotism is condemned in Scripture or if it provides Satan an opportunity to influence us, the Christian is well-advised to avoid it.

Some compare hypnosis (especially self-hypnosis) with deep Christian meditation and intense prayer. They compare the hypnotic trance with the examples of trances and visionary states in the Bible (Acts 10:10). Some claim that to equate hypnosis with false religions and demon possession is to confuse the practice of hypnosis with the purpose of hypnosis. If hypnosis is a Biblical tool that can draw us closer to God, refresh our mind, and open ourselves to His instruction, the Christian would be well-advised to practice it.

Some see hypnosis as a powerful tool to help get rid of bad habits, to establish good habits, to build confidence, lose weight, or to have pain-free dental work. Others say that instead of looking inward for our help that we should look to God. The spiritual dimension of hypnosis will likely cause introductory psychology courses to dismiss hypnosis as an interesting, but not very important phenomena or as a cool parlor trick. For the Christian student of psychology, it is much more.

Meditation

What is meditation? In introductory psychology courses you will be told that meditation is a form of deep concentration in which the mind is focused on a single thing or emptied of thought. You will be told that meditation is the practice of calming the mind and focusing attention. You will be introduced to various techniques of meditation. In Sunday school, from the pulpit, or in your personal study, you may have learned that meditation is a practice commanded by Scripture. You learned that meditation means concentrating on God, focusing on His Word, listening for God's voice, and reflecting on His works and His will.

Assignment 10.4

Read *Meditation: A Requirement* by Helen E. Martin at:

http://www.asa3.org/aSA/PSCF/1979/JASA6-79Martin.html

In introductory psychology courses you may learn about the benefits of Transcendental Meditation (TM), Hindu meditation, Bahá'í meditation, Buddhist meditation, Vipassana Meditation, Tafakkur, body scan meditation, and more. You may learn that meditation will help you enhance awareness and gain more control of physical and mental processes, that you can get in touch with your inner-self, that you will experience higher states of consciousness, or that you will to connect to your spirit guide. You may be told that religious beliefs (worldview) are not important, that meditation is about consciousness. Do not believe it. It is all about religious beliefs and worldviews.

In introductory psychology courses, you will learn that mediation is associated with long-term effects such as improved physical and mental health and reduced stress. There is research indicating tangible benefits for most varieties of meditation; including Christian meditation. The Christian student studying psychology must carefully evaluate those benefits and the means by which they are attained.

Psychoactive Drugs

Psychoactive or **psychotropic** drugs alter consciousness, behavior, cognition, and emotions. Since ancient times people have used psychoactive drugs to create hallucinations, relieve pain, and alter consciousness. Some drugs (like caffeine, tobacco, and alcohol) are so widely accepted that many do not think of them as drugs. Others (opiates, cocaine, marijuana) carry severe legal restrictions. **Psychopharmacology** is the study of the relationships between drugs and mental processes. Psychopharmacology addresses illegal (**illicit**) and legal (**licit**) drugs. This text will review licit psychoactive drugs in a later chapter.

Because caffeine, nicotine, and alcohol are psychoactive drugs, it is probably safe to say that very few people today have not at some time used psychoactive drugs. But every day millions of people **abuse** psychoactive drugs. The cost to society, families, and individuals from psychoactive drug abuse is staggering. This section will discuss the categories of psychoactive drugs and the basic processes and factors affecting their use.

Assignment 10.5
Read NIDA InfoFacts: Costs to Society at

http://www.nida.nih.gov/Infofacts/costs.html

Psychoactive drugs work by crossing the blood/brain barrier and altering the way neurotransmitters work. Psychoactive drugs may cause more or less of a neurotransmitter to be released, block the reception of a neurotransmitter, or block reabsorption of a neurotransmitter. Several factors impact the effect of a drug. Drug effects vary according to the amount of the drug ingested, the drug's potency, the route of administration, the user's previous experience and expectation, the users age, body weight, and mood, and the environment in which the drug is used.

Regular use of a drug may lead to tolerance. **Tolerance** refers to decreased susceptibility to the same quantity of a drug. A drug user who over time requires more of a drug to achieve the same effect is developing a tolerance to the drug. With continued use, drug users may develop **dependence** (commonly known as **addiction**). Someone who is drug dependent

For your consideration:

Is there a difference between drug use and drug abuse? Is there a difference between alcohol use and alcohol abuse? Is there a difference between caffeine use and caffeine abuse? If so, what is the difference?

experiences very unpleasant physical and/or emotional symptoms when not using the drug **(withdrawal)**. Those symptoms are so unpleasant that the person compulsively seeks and uses the drug despite obvious and serious consequences. Researchers differentiate between psychological and physiological (physical) dependence. In **psychological dependence** the user experiences mental or emotional discomfort when not using the drug. In **physiological dependence** the user experiences physical symptoms when not using the drug (i.e. seizures, diarrhea, and pain). The physical and psychological withdrawal symptoms are often the direct opposite of the effects of using the drug. Some drugs are more addictive (produce dependence more often and faster) than others. Heroin and methamphetamine are very addictive.

Christians studying psychopharmacology must reconcile the Christian view of sin and personal responsibility with research indicating genetic and environmental influences on drug abuse and dependence.

Modern psychologists must reconcile their view that substance dependence is a genetic-based disease with research indicating that strong religious beliefs are associated with low levels of drug abuse and dependence.

Researchers usually classify illicit psychoactive drugs into four categories:

- Depressants (Sedative-hypnotics): Depressants slow down (depress) the central nervous system and sedate, calm, relax, and cause sleep.
- Stimulants: Stimulants stimulate the central nervous system and increase alertness, reduce fatigue, and elevate mood.
- Opiates (Narcotics): Opiates are derivatives of opium and used to reduce pain.
- Hallucinogens (Psychedelics): Hallucinogens distort perceptions of reality, thought processes, and produce hallucinations.

Depressants: Alcohol

Alcohol (ethanol) is the most familiar and most widely abused drug in our society. Alcohol is a bulky drug, requiring considerably larger doses than most other drugs. A common perception of alcohol is that it is a stimulant. Alcohol is a depressant, not a stimulant. Another perception about alcohol is that, in small doses, it reduces inhibitions and enhances social interactions. One reason that alcohol reduces inhibitions is that people expect it to have that effect. Research has shown that people who think they are drinking alcohol (but who really are not) behave as though they were actually drinking alcohol. Subjects were less inhibited and more relaxed. Another reason may be that by depressing the inhibitory functions of the brain, people behave in ways they would not otherwise. We may perceive dis-inhibition as stimulating. The perceived social benefits of dis-inhibition stand in contrasted to the extreme negative consequences of dis-inhibition (violence, rape, and a host of risky behaviors).

As the dose of alcohol increases, psychological functioning declines. First, complex cognitive abilities decline (planning, problem solving, memory). Next (and in order), fine motor skills (driving, writing, working with the hands), gross motor skills (walking), and involuntary motor activity (reacting to pain, breathing) are disrupted. Alcohol overdose can cause blackouts (amnesia of events while intoxicated) and death.

Alcohol metabolizes in the liver. Liver disease is the most likely consequence of chronic alcohol use. Chronic alcohol use also contributes to cognitive (learning and memory) and motor deficits. It has been associated with brain shrinkage, sexual dysfunction, increased risk for injury.

> **Metabolism is the body's process of converting drugs into other substances for eventual excretion from the body.**

Depressants: Sedative – Hypnotics

Sedative-hypnotics (also known as tranquilizers) reduce the activity level of neurons. There are many types of sedative-hypnotics and most affect the neurotransmitter **gamma-amino butyric acid** (GABA). Hypnotics change brainwave activity from predominately alpha and beta waves (characteristic of wakefulness and alertness) to delta and theta waves (characteristic of rest and sleep). In many cases the effects of hypnotics are indistinguishable from alcohol. Sluggish movement, relaxed muscles, and a sleepy state of consciousness are characteristic of sedative-hypnotics.

Many sedatives-hypnotics are **potentiated** by alcohol. Potentiation means that in combination, alcohol and sedative-hypnotics produce an exponentially greater effect.

As noted earlier, withdrawal effects often are the opposite of the effect of the drug itself. Withdrawal from sedative-hypnotics (which slow brain activity) may lead to seizures (out-of-control brain activity)

Stimulants

By mimicking adrenaline, stimulants decrease reaction time, increase heart rate, heighten mood, increase vigilance and alertness, and reduce fatigue. Stimulants also may cause nervousness, jittery movements, insomnia, irregular heartbeats, and anxiety or panic.

Stimulants: Caffeine

Caffeine is the most widely used psychoactive drug is the world. Your morning coffee or tea, lunchtime soda, and chocolate snack all contain caffeine. Two cups of coffee (approximately 150 mg of caffeine) generally produces mood-elevating and fatigue-relieving effects. Large doses may produce insomnia, restlessness, and anxiety. Caffeine may raise blood pressure slightly.

College students sometimes take caffeine pills to stay awake to study. Caffeine pills contain a high dose of the drug and may produce symptoms of anxiety, nervousness, fear, and palpitations in people who are not accustomed to high doses. Caffeine users who require high doses of the drug to experience its effect have developed a tolerance to caffeine.

Stimulants: Amphetamine & Methamphetamine

The amphetamine molecule was first synthesized in the late 1800's. American and Japanese pilots used amphetamines extensively during World War II. Low doses of amphetamine increased energy, concentration, alertness, mood, and decreased the need for sleep. Today, amphetamine and related drugs are used to treat asthma, narcolepsy, obesity, and attention deficit disorder.

Amphetamines were the primary drugs of abuse from the 1940s to the 1970s. Beginning in the 1990s, amphetamine use resurged (in the form of methamphetamine) and has reached epidemic proportions. The **capture ratio** (the percentage of users who develop dependence) for amphetamines is very high. The feelings of euphoria and high self-confidence from methamphetamine are so strong that many methamphetamine users report symptoms of dependence after just one use. Tolerance to amphetamines builds quickly so users require ever increasing doses to achieve the desired effect.

Symptoms of amphetamine use include rapid speech, dilated pupils, increased energy and goal directed activity, mood swings, irritability, nervousness, chest pains, palpitations, and sweating. Signs of long term use include confusion, neglecting school, work, and social activities, aggressiveness and violence, wild mood swings, significant weight loss, sores on face and arms, diarrhea, vomiting, hallucinations, paranoia, tremors, convulsions, long periods of sleeplessness followed by long periods of sleep, and tooth decay from the inside out. Long-term administration of amphetamine produces hallucinations and delusions indistinguishable from schizophrenia.

For further information:

PBS produced a documentary on methamphetamine available for viewing on-line at http://www.pbs.org/wgbh/pages/frontline/meth/

Stimulants: Cocaine

For centuries, South American Indians used cocoa leaves to increase endurance and reduce fatigue and hunger. Cocaine was first isolated from cocoa leaves in the mid 1800s. After personally testing its effects, Sigmund Freud became one of the early proponents of cocaine's antidepressant effects. Cocaine has been used as a treatment for asthma, colic, and as an anesthetic in eye surgery. Cocaine is usually snorted but a high-potency crystalline form (crack cocaine) is smoked.

Rhesus monkeys were allowed to choose between intravenous injections of cocaine and food as reinforcement for pressing a lever. The choice between cocaine and food was available every 15 minutes for 8 days. The animals chose cocaine almost exclusively, which resulted in high cocaine intake, decreased food intake, weight loss, and erratic behavior. The study provided evidence of the reinforcing effect of cocaine (Aigner & Balster, 1978).

Cocaine's effects on neurotransmitters are similar to those of amphetamines, so its effects on humans and its potential for dependence are also similar. Initially cocaine was thought to be non-addictive, but its capture ratio is near that of methamphetamine. Because cocaine acts on the same area of the brain (the limbic system) that is activated when we experience love, pride, and sex, it provides powerful reinforcement.

Low doses of cocaine produce feelings of euphoria, increased energy, arousal, alertness, and decreased need for sleep. High doses produce irritability, anxiety, and paranoia. Cocaine, like other amphetamines, produces a **"rebound effect."** When the drug euphoria ends, users may suffer a rebound depression that can lead to suicidal thoughts or attempts. The rebound effect may explain why long-term cocaine users report that they need the drug to "just feel normal." Long-term use is related to hallucinations, severe irritability, damaged social functioning, paranoia, seizures, headaches, and tremors. Recent research suggests that cocaine use increases the risk for brain aneurysms.

Stimulants: Nicotine

Like cocaine was first administered by chewing cocoa leaves, nicotine was first administered by chewing tobacco leaves. Today people deliver nicotine to their brains by smoking, chewing, or sniffing tobacco.

Nicotine has a high capture ratio; one-third to one-half of people who try nicotine become regular users and most nicotine users begin as adolescents. Today, more than 3.5 million teenagers use tobacco. Like the other stimulants, nicotine increases dopamine levels in the limbic system to produce mild euphoria, increased alertness, and increased energy.

Each year nearly half a million Americans die from tobacco use. Tobacco use is strongly associated with cancer, emphysema, heart disease, and strokes. One of every six deaths in the United States is related to smoking tobacco, making tobacco more lethal than all other addictive drugs combined.

> **For additional information about amphetamines, cocaine, and other stimulants, visit the Drug Enforcement Administration's Drugs of Abuse Publications Home at http://www.usdoj.gov/dea/pubs/abuse/index.htm**

Opiates

Opiates (narcotics) are some of the oldest drugs used by humans. Opium is extracted from the poppy plant. Opium derivatives (heroin, morphine, codeine, oxycodone, and hydrocodone) and synthetic opiates are powerful painkillers. They resemble endorphins, our body's natural painkilling and stress reducing substance.

Opiates are useful to treat pain, suppress coughs, alleviate diarrhea, and as an anesthetic. As a drug of abuse, opiates are ingested orally, smoked, sniffed, or injected. In addition to alleviating pain, opiates produce feelings of euphoria and reduce feelings of anxiety and aggression. Opiate abuse is associated with drowsiness, decreased concentration and motivation, constipation, nausea, vomiting, and decreased respiration. The long-term dangers of opiate abuse include infection, disease, overdose, adulterants in street drugs, and non-sterile administration (dirty needles).

Opiates are highly addictive and users may develop a strong tolerance. After months of heavy use, some users may administer many times the dosage that would kill a non-tolerant user. A rebound effect, similar to the stimulants, requires dependent users to take the drug to "just feel normal." Symptoms of opiate withdrawal are so severe (pain, depression, diarrhea, chills, restlessness, and insomnia) that recovery rates from opiate dependence are low. Methadone (a long acting opiate) has allowed many to avoid withdrawal symptoms and resume some normal social behavior.

> **For additional information about Opiates, visit the Drug Enforcement Administration's Drugs of Abuse Publications Home at http://www.usdoj.gov/dea/pubs/abuse/index.htm**

Hallucinogens

Hallucinogens are a class of psychoactive drugs that produce **hallucinations** (sensory or perceptual experiences that occur without any external stimulus), **depersonalization** (an altered perception in which one feels detached from oneself), sensory disturbances, thought disturbances, and mood changes. Common hallucinogens are LSD, MDMA (ecstasy), mescaline, psilocybin, and ketamine.

Hallucinogens: LSD

Dr. Albert Hoffman first synthesized LSD (lysergic acid diethylamide or "acid") in 1938. In 1943 he accidentally discovered its psychoactive properties when he absorbed a small about of the drug through his finger. LSD is the most powerful psychoactive substance known. Thousandths of a gram produce powerful effects.

LSD produces a wide variety of psychological experiences. Users report deep religious feelings, sexual feelings, sadness, anxiety, and fear. Users experience bizarre thoughts and beliefs (**delusions**) like believing they can fly or can stop a train by stepping in front of it. Sometimes users report deep new insights into themselves or the nature of the universe (those "insights" contributed to LSD's reputation as a "mind-expanding" drug). Perceptual alterations include distortions of vision, sound, taste, smell, touch, and an altered perception of time. Some report **synesthesia,** the experience of a sensation by different sensory process ("seeing" a smell or "tasting" a sound). Many report vivid hallucinations. Occasionally the experience is extremely frightening (a "bad trip"). Some users report **flashbacks** (brief episodes similar to the drug-induced state) weeks or months after using the drug. Physical reactions include dilated pupils, low body temperature, nausea, sweating, and increased heart rate.

LSD was used in the early 1950s in research on psychosis, to make patients "more open" to psychoanalysis, and in the treatment of drug dependence. It was even used to treat anxiety and depression in cancer patients. Beginning in the 1960s, the "hippie" counter-culture, led by Dr. Timothy Leary, used LSD to "turn on, tune it, and drop out." The drug became an icon for a new-age worldview that placed great value on self-fulfillment, experimentation with drugs, and a sexual "revolution."

> **For additional information about LSD and other hallucinogens, visit the Drug Enforcement Administration's Drugs of Abuse Publications Home at http://www.usdoj.gov/dea/pubs/abuse/index.htm**

Marijuana

The leaves and buds of the marijuana (**cannabis**) plant have been smoked, brewed, and eaten as an intoxicant and medicinal herb for centuries. Marijuana is in a category by itself because it does not resemble the other classes of drugs in structure or effect. The active ingredient in marijuana is **delta-4-tetrahydrocannabinol (THC)**. Hashish is a concentrated form of cannabis resin. Marijuana is the most frequently used illicit drug in the world.

Low doses of marijuana produce a sense of well-being, relaxation, alterations in thinking, enhanced appetite, and enhanced perceptions of sight, smell, taste, and hearing (colors may seem brighter, music more vivid, humor more funny). Low doses also increase heart rate, cause "dry mouth," red eyes, and poor concentration ("stoned"). Higher doses produce more significant alterations in cognition, rapidly changing emotions, anxiety and paranoia, impaired memory, and hallucinations. Chronic use is said to lead to **amotivational syndrome** (apathy, poor judgment, memory and concentration deficits, and a general lack of motivation). Marijuana smoke contains a number of toxins and carcinogens. Chronic users may suffer bronchitis, emphysema, and bronchial asthma.

For further information:

Visit the National Institute on Drug Abuse (NIDA) *InfoFacts: Science-Based Facts on Drug Abuse and Addiction* **at http://www.nida.nih.gov/Infofacts/Infofaxindex.html**

Chapter 11

Cogito, ergo sum (I think, therefore I am)- René Descartes

Language and Cognition

When we use language and when think we engage in very complex, multi-faceted, and interdependent mental processes. Language, memory, and cognition are not independent activities. They can be examined one by one, but to rigidly distinguish one from the others is to begin down a reductive path. Language, memory, and cognitive ability are unique to humans, part of our God-likeness, and necessary for our relatedness to God. Introductory psychology courses, in their naturalistic tradition, present language, memory, and cognition as distinct mental processes, each with its own evolutionary development and purpose, and solely in terms of physical processes.

Language

The use of language is uniquely human. Language is a set of symbols (sounds, gestures, or written characters) used to represent objects (actions, events, and ideas) according to a set of rules. Symbols allow us to describe objects that are in another place, events that occurred at a different time, and to describe abstract concepts.

Humans in all cultures go through roughly the same stages of language development even though children grow up in widely different cultures. Children develop language skills almost effortlessly. Children who have not been exposed to

Researchers have described interesting accounts of primates acquiring language. Kanzi, a chimpanzee at the Great Ape Trust, reportedly has a "vocabulary" of more than 500 words and the ability to comprehend human speech. His comprehension is said to be equal to that of a two-and-a-half-year-old child. Kanzi uses symbols to make requests and is said to "speak" with humans via a keyboard attached to a voice synthesizer. Kanzi's abilities are said to have implications on the understanding of human evolution. Many argue that Kanzi is demonstrating conditioned behaviors that do not constitute language. Others note that primates' use of structure and syntax falls short of that of a two-year-old child.

a language make one up. Many introductory psychology texts cite these observations as evidence that language acquisition is an innate biologically directed process. A biological explanation for language acquisition is necessary for a comprehensive evolutionary description of Mankind, but not necessarily correct. A Christian view of language acquisition must acknowledge that language is an innate and unique gift from God to Mankind and a crucial part of our relationship with Him, but does not necessarily concede that it is solely biological.

For further information about Kanzi, read the article *Speaking Bonobo* at http://www.smithsonianmag.com/science-nature/10022981.html

---

Language is composed of phonemes, morphemes, phrases, and sentences, arranged hierarchically to communicate meaning. **Phonemes** are the smallest distinguishable sounds in a language. The sound of the letter "t" is a phoneme. There are about 44 phonemes in the English language. The letter "t" corresponds to a single phoneme. Some consonants, all vowels, and some combinations of letters correspond to more than one phoneme. **Morphemes** are the smallest meaningful units in a language. Morphemes are usually whole words but may be parts of words such as prefixes, suffixes, and word stems. **Syntax** is the system of rules that govern how words form phrases and sentences.

The scientific study of language began in the late 1950's with Noam Chomsky. Before Chomsky, Skinnerian behaviorism provided the predominant theory of language acquisition.

**Assignment 11.1
Read Genesis 11:1-9**

Skinner (as you might have guessed) believed that language was nothing more than behaviors learned through principles of conditioning. Chomsky believed that the principles of conditioning were insufficient to explain the speed at which children acquire language, the nearly infinite number of ways children combine words into sentences, and the common syntax errors children make (errors that are not modeled or reinforced by parents). Chomsky's theory suggested that humans have an inborn mental structure (**Language Acquisition Device**) that is pre-programmed with a set of rules about language (**Universal Grammar**). According to Chomsky's theory, we are born "hard-wired" with a universal grammar that makes us receptive to the commonalities of all languages. Our hard-wiring allows us to easily learn any language if it is consistent with the universal grammar. Chomsky believed that language has an evolutionary explanation but struggled to explain the incredibly creative ways we use language. Today, most researchers believe that our innate capacity for language develops in conjunction with interaction with others. Language learning begins in the womb as the developing baby hears language. Many parents speak to their unborn child through the womb. Babies respond to speech at birth, but from 0 to 4 months, babies communicate the only way they can; by crying.

Until they are about 3 months old, babies respond to phonemes from any language. After about 3 months, babies respond better to sounds from the language they hear most often. At around 3 months, babies begin to produce vocal sounds and at around 6 months, they babble and make sounds that resemble the phonemes of many different languages. By babbling, babies practice the sounds, the intonations, and the rhythms of language, and learn to modulate their voice. Babbling also becomes a new way for the baby to express its needs and wants. As the baby develops, the babbling sounds more like phonemes from the language the baby hears. Deaf babies babble with their hands. Between about 9 and 13 months, children begin to produce simple single words (**holophrases**) to express feelings or desires. The child may use the same holophrase to describe many things and adults are likely to interpret the holophrase as a full sentence.

> **A child may say "dog" to mean dog, cat, or chicken. Mom and dad will interpret "dog" to mean I see a dog, give me the dog, or where is the dog?**

At about two years old, children begin to combine two or three words to make short sentences. The sentences are **telegraphic**, meaning the sentence does not contain articles or prepositions.

> **A child using telegraphic speech might say "go potty" to mean "I need to go to the bathroom."**

We learn to comprehend language (**receptive language**) faster than we learn to produce it (**expressive language**). As a three year old, you understood far more than you could say. The same is true for learning a second language. Your ability to understand a new language develops faster than your ability to speak it.

By about age three, children begin to use tenses and plurals, but tend to over **generalize** the rules of syntax. We continue to develop language ability throughout childhood as we learn the complexities and subtleties of the language.

> **A child who says "I do gooder" is over generalizing the rule that says adding an –er (tall/taller, big/bigger) indicates one thing is more than another.**

As you probably know from personal experience, language comprehension is complicated by a language's ambiguity. Ambiguity, in terms of language, means that the same words can have more than one meaning or can be understood in more than one way. Language acquisition involves learning to merge context and meaning. Research indicates that in the absence of context, we choose the most common or personally relevant meaning for ambiguous term.

Homonyms and homophones are examples of ambiguity in language.

Homonyms are words that sound alike but have different meanings.	*Homophones* are a type of homonym that *sound* alike, have different meanings, and have different spellings.
Please polish the Polish table. He could lead if he got the lead out. The farm used to produce produce. The dump was full so it had to refuse more refuse. Let's present the present. When shot at, the dove dove into the bushes. The bandage was wound around the wound. They were too close to the door to close it. The buck does funny things when the does are present. I had to subject the subject to a series of tests.	Breathe the air. He is heir to the throne. Walk down the aisle. I'll do in tomorrow. That is not allowed. Read it aloud. That band is banned. The wind really blew. His eyes are blue. Use the parking brake. I am tired, I need a break. Say bye so we can run by the store to buy some milk. My nose knows the smell of mom's fresh bread. It is not right to write, about the tribe's ancient rite.

Cognition

What is thinking? How do we think? What goes on in the brain when we think? What strategies do we use to solve problems and make decisions? How do psychologists explain creativity? These are some of the issues that cognitive psychology seeks to answer.

Introductory psychology texts' definitions of cognition vary greatly. For our purposes, cognition is the mental process of thinking, problem solving, and creativity. The study of cognition explores the ways we use and manipulate mental representations of objects, actions, events, and ideas. When we think about dogs, fishing, death, green, or love, we are using **concepts**. Cognition involves constructing concepts to describe the sensory world. It involves constructing concepts to understand the spoken and written word. Cognition also involves coordinating movement and behavior to accomplish goals.

Advances in brain scanning technology allow researchers to monitor the brain activity of subjects engaged in cognitive activity. Research indicates that some parts of the brain are highly specialized and perform specific cognitive tasks but most cognition involves more than one area of the brain. To us, thinking feels like a single action, but actually, it is the coordinated effort of different parts of the brain. The coordination takes place in the prefrontal cortex, the part of your brain right behind your eyes. That coordination, or executive process, is uniquely human. Introductory psychology texts will probably state that the prefrontal cortex is the most highly evolved structure in the human brain. The executive process plans, guides, and organizes the activity of the specialized parts.

The term "**cognitive style**" refers to the way in which you usually (habitually) think. Your specific cognitive style is unique to you, but most people are either analytic or holistic thinkers. **Analytic thinkers (field independent)** tend to break down complexities into component parts or steps and to process information in a detailed step-by-step approach. **Holistic thinkers (field dependent)** tend to look at the "big picture." Holistic thinkers tend not to process information in terms of component parts and steps. Instead, they work with overall meaning and purpose.

Attention refers to our ability to concentrate on one thing while ignoring others. **Selective attention** refers to our ability to process information from one part of the environment and to exclude others. Research indicates that we focus our attention on a limited amount of information at any given time, but that information that is not the focus of attention is processed at an unconscious level. Concentration is a very focused form of attention in which we ignore anything that does not lead to a particular cognitive objective.

Decision-making involves evaluating and choosing between alternatives. In an **additive decision-making** strategy, we weigh the benefits of each alternative, assign value to each benefit, add the benefits, and choose the alternative with the most relative benefit. In an **elimination decision-making** strategy, alternatives are eliminated if they fail to meet pre-determined criteria.

Problem solving is one of the most complex of all human mental activities. We spend tremendous mental energy solving problems. In fact, some researchers suggest that all thought is, at some level, problem solving.

Creativity (divergent thinking) is the ability to generate novel ideas or concepts or to generate new associations between existing ideas and concepts. The ancient Greeks believed inspiration (creativity) was a gift from the Muses. Modern neurobiologists suggest that highly creative people differ from less creative people in terms of the neurotransmitters dopamine and serotonin.

Researchers suggest a relationship between creativity and bipolar disorder. Evolutionary psychologists ask how our creative capacity evolved and point to cave drawing and tool making as the dawning of human creativity. Humanist psychologists examine the characteristics of creative people and suggest strategies to increase creativity. Social psychologists seek to discover the environments and experiences associated with creativity. Christian psychologists should not lose sight that creativity is a gift from God and a part of our God-likeness.

Cognitive Development

Cognitive development refers to the ways in which our thinking, problem solving, decision-making, and creative abilities develop from childhood through adolescence to adulthood.

The theorist best known for research on cognitive development is Jean Piaget. Piaget theorized that our thinking develops through stages as we mature and explore our surroundings. Piaget named the period from birth to about 2 years the **sensorimotor stage**. Cognitive development at this stage is a function of sensations and motor activities. During this stage, infants discover relationships between their bodies and the environment and begin to develop **schemas** (mental representations of objects and relationships). Infants discover that they can control their bodies and move objects (**causality**). Early in this stage, children act as though an object hidden from sight ceases to exist. Later in this stage, children understand **object permanence** and will search for hidden objects.

Piaget named the period from age 2 to about age 7 the **preoperational stage.** In this stage children begin to use language and symbols. In the preoperational stage, memory and imagination begin to develop. During this stage, children begin to pretend and role-play. Their thinking is **non-logical** and **egocentric** (a Freudian term meaning unable to take the point of view of other people). Children in this stage believe that everything that exists has some kind of consciousness (**animism**).

In the **concrete operational stage** (7 to 11 years), children develop the ability to think logically about concrete objects. Before this stage, children's perceptions of objects are dominated by the appearance of the object. For example, when shown the same volume of liquid poured into two containers, one short and wide and the other tall and thin, the child believes that the tall thin container holds more liquid. The child believes that there are more blocks when blocks are spread out than when the same blocks are in a small pile. In the concrete operational stage, the child develops **conservation**, the ability to recognize different aspects of an object. Egocentric thought and belief in animism diminish in this stage.

Piaget's fourth stage of cognitive development is the **formal operational stage** (from 11 years to adulthood). This stage is characterized by the ability to think logically, to plan complex behavior, to speculate, and to formulate hypotheses and to systematically test them. The ability to think abstractly allows adolescents to operate outside of the limits of concrete objects, to use symbols, and to evaluate ideas, emotions, concepts, and hypothetical situations.

Piaget was a philosopher and an epistemologist. He did not claim to be an educational psychologist, but his work on cognitive development is foundational to teacher education programs today. Before Piaget, psychologists believed that children were just miniature adults and that they shared the same thought processes as adults. Piaget's work has been criticized for a number of reasons. His theory is based on observations of a small number of children from well-educated and affluent families. Piaget thought that inherent forces propelled children invariably and automatically from one stage to the next. Research suggests however, that environmental forces play an important role in cognitive development. Subsequent research suggested that the stages are not as distinct and sequential as Piaget thought and that he underestimated children's abilities. Piaget's work on cognitive development has not been subject to significant criticism from the Church (his work on moral development is another story). His theories have influenced Christian education from the Church nursery and Sunday school class to the Christian schools and universities, despite the fact that the man was a naturalist and humanist. Keep that in mind.

"If it weren't for caffeine I'd have no personality whatsoever!" — Anonymous

Personality

What is personality? In everyday language, we say that someone who is outgoing and charming has "a lot of personality." In psychology, definitions of personality vary. An early researcher catalogued almost 50 different definitions. For our purposes, personality is a system of **enduring inner characteristics that contribute to consistency in our thoughts, feelings, and behaviors.**

Remember that the goals of psychology are to observe and describe, suggest meaning, predict, and to improve or change. In pursuit of those goals, psychologists have proposed personality theories from the biological, behavioral, cognitive, psychoanalytic, and humanistic perspectives. As you will see in the next section, each perspective also led to different approaches to explaining and caring for mental pain.

Theories suggest meaning. Theories seek to describe laws that explain why we observe what we observe. They are built in the context of the theorist's worldview. For the Christian, any acceptable personality theory must be consistent with a Christian worldview. As we have learned throughout this text, the dominant perspectives in psychology do not adequately consider God, sin, redemption, freedom, responsibility, and absolute moral laws. The Christian studying psychology may however, learn and understand what psychologists have observed and the theories that propose to explain personality.

Personality is a system of enduring inner traits that contribute to consistency in our thoughts, feelings, and behaviors. A **trait** is a consistent psychological characteristic. Shyness is a trait. Peace, longsuffering, kindness, goodness, faithfulness, gentleness, and self-control are traits (Galatians 5:22,23).

Traits exist on a continuum or in degrees. You may be gentler than I. I may be shyer than you. We can describe people as high or low in a particular trait. Individual differences are the essence of personalities. If we rate someone on a number of individual personality traits, we begin to see a personality profile (personality type). **Personality types** are collections of traits that occur together in some individuals. Macho types, hippies, Goths, and geeks are examples of personality types. Traits are relatively enduring, meaning that they are stable over time. Relatively enduring is not to say that they are fixed and unchangeable. A **state**, however, is by definition short-lived. One who is generally calm can, depending on circumstance, be in a very anxious state.

Using factor analysis, psychologists sought to discover the basic dimensions (factors) that make up a personality. Factor analysis is a statistical technique used in personality research to discover the basic components common to all personalities (remember that traits exist on a continuum). Several researchers, operating independently and studying different populations began to discover similar personality patterns. Today, most psychologists believe that personality can be well described in terms of five traits (the "Big Five").

The **Big Five** factors of personality;

- Extroverted versus Introverted
- Agreeable versus Antagonistic
- Conscientious versus Negligent
- Emotionally stable versus Emotionally unstable
- Open to new experiences/ideas versus Closed to new experiences/ideas

With observations indicating that five factors make up the basis of our personality, researchers have proposed thousands of theories to explain how personality develops. The psychoanalytic perspective theorizes that childhood experiences and unconscious conflicts shape our personality development. Theories from a behavioral perspective explain personality development in terms of traits that are strengthened through reinforcement. The humanistic theories suggest that innate forces shape and equip us to reach our full potential. Cognitive theories trace our personality to our cognitive efforts to make sense of and influence our environment. The biological perspective produced explanations of personality development in terms of genetic and evolutionary influences.

> **Evolutionary psychology (also known as sociobiology) is an evolutionary approach to understanding human nature.**

Interesting studies on identical twins suggest that genetic factors do play an important role in personality. During a time when adoption agencies often separated identical twins, researchers studied identical twins separated at birth and raised by different families in different cultures. One large study found that although identical twins differ in many ways (intelligence skills, abilities, preferences, thinking styles), personalities were strikingly similar.

Personality Tests

With the knowledge that there is universality to personality traits, researchers developed tests to determine individuals' personality types. Previously, psychological tests had been limited to educational tests to assess knowledge, intelligence, and to place students in the right level in school. Personality tests were used initially to help therapists discover personality traits and to guide treatment. Today there are literally thousands of tests linking personality traits with other aspects of behavior or to predict performance or behavior.

One of the early personality tests was the famous Rorschach (inkblot) test. In the **Rorschach test**, subjects were shown a series of inkblots and asked to interpret the "scene." Rorschach noted that people projected their own mental processes to the blots. After collecting data on thousands of tests, researchers were able to correlate certain test results with various personality types and mental and disorders.

A subsequent test, the **Minnesota Multiphasic Personality Inventory (MMPI)**, was designed to make predictions about mental disorders. People with known mental conditions were given a large battery of true/false questions. Their responses were compared to "normal" people. Questions that discriminated between people with mental disorders and those without mental disorders were included in the MMPI. A score above a certain level on a particular scale indicated a response pattern like that of people with known mental problems and perhaps indicated a need for treatment. Today the MMPI-2 has 10 clinical scales that psychologists use to identify emotional, personal, social, or behavioral problems and to aid in treatment planning. The MMPI contains five validity scales that gauge the accuracy of the clinical scales (test-takers who lie or try to fool the examiner).

The Myer-Briggs Type Indicator (MBTI) is the most popular personality test in use today. The MBTI's premise is that we usually think and act according to our personality type. The MBTI describes ways of thinking and acting in terms of 16 possible combinations of 4 dichotomous preferences. The 4 dichotomies are:

- Extraversion (E) vs. Introversion (I)
- Sensing (S) vs. Intuition (N)
- Thinking (T) vs. Feeling (F)
- Judging (J) vs. Perceiving (P)

The extraversion/introversion scale indicates whether you prefer to focus your energy on the outer world of people and things or on your own inner world of ideas and beliefs.

The sensing/intuition scale indicates how you prefer to process information. Do you prefer to focus clearly on basic factual information (S) or do you prefer ideas, interpretation, and meaning (N)?

The thinking/feeling scale indicates how you prefer to make decisions. A "T" indicates a preference for objective logic and consistency. An "F" reflects a preference for emotions and circumstances.

The judging/perceiving scale indicates how you structure and organize information. Do you prefer to plan and make decisions (J) or to be flexible and open to changes (P)?

MBTI Type Indicators			
ISTJ	ISFJ	INFJ	INTJ
ISTP	ISFP	INFP	INTP
ESTP	ESFP	ENFP	ENTP
ESTJ	ESFJ	ENFJ	ENTJ

The MBTI is grounded in Carl Jung's personality theories. Jung's theories (discussed below) lead some Christians to reject the MBTI for its "pagan and occult" foundations. For more information visit http://www.psychoheresy-aware.org/bksonline.html to download *Four Temperaments, Astrology & Personality Testing*

Theories of Personality: Sigmund Freud

Sigmund Freud proposed modern psychology's first major personality theory. Many subsequent theories were developed in response to Freud. Like Charles Darwin's impact on the modern study of biology, no one has had more effect on modern psychology than Sigmund Freud. His theories influence most academic and professional disciplines. The vocabulary of his theory is a part of common language today. Like Charles

Darwin, Freud's personality theory and psychoanalytic counseling are the focus of severe criticism by Christians.

Freud's theory presumed God does not exist. It was deterministic and it emphasized sex and aggression as the prime motivations for human behavior and personality development. With such foundational worldview-level differences of opinion, the Christian criticisms are not surprising. Freud's theory lacked empirical evidence. With such a foundational world-view level difference of opinion, criticisms by naturalist psychologists are not surprising.

You will be taught Darwin's theory in college. You will be taught Freud's theories in college. Please do not forget that understanding the material and accepting the worldview are different. You can do one without the other (You would be well-served by reading *How to Stay Christian in College* by J. Budziszewski).

Freud described personality in terms of three components: the **id,** the **ego,** and the **super-ego**. According to Freud, the majority of mental functions were unconscious. Freud described the Id as primitive, animal-like, irrational, pleasure seeking, unconscious, and selfish. Children, were are said to be "all id." Some suggested that the id was a metaphor for the "primitive" limbic system.

Freud thought that sexual and aggressive impulses were the source of our mental energy (**libido**).

Freud described the **ego** as our "sense of self." Many equate the ego with the executive functions of the frontal cortex. The ego, like the prefrontal cortex, was said to plan and coordinate mental processes. The ego consciously restrains impulses, directs the libido, and defends us against painful thoughts and memories (**repression**). Anxiety is the result of the ego's incomplete repression of troubling thoughts, memories, and impulses. According to Freud, if we exert too much energy repressing the id, we become depressed.

Assignment 12.1

Define and memorize the definitions of

Id
Ego
Super-ego
(You do not have to agree with Freud's theories, but these terms will be on a test someday.)

Assignment 12.2

Define:

Anal stage
Denial
Displacement
Genital Stage
Latency stage
Oral stage
Phallic stage
Projection
Reaction formation
Regression
Sublimation
Suppression

Freudian psychotherapy focuses on bringing repressed problems to conscious awareness, thereby freeing-up energy for productive living.

The **super-ego** operates like a supervisor of the mind. As we are taught morals and values, the super-ego internalizes those morals and values and applies them to our behavior. In Freud's theory, it is the super-ego's expression of parental values (not the Holy Spirit) that convicts us when we err.

According to Freud, we use **defense mechanisms** to avoid consciously confronting troublesome thoughts, memories, and impulses. Defense mechanisms are unconscious ego-defense mechanisms. Denial, rationalization, intellectualization, projection, displacement, reaction formation, sublimation, and regression are each defense mechanisms that subconsciously lessen anxiety.

- **Denial** is refusing to admit something has happened.
- **Rationalization** is providing an explanation for behavior that you subconsciously know is false.
- **Intellectualization** describes taking a detached, rational, and logical approach to emotionally uncomfortable issues.
- **Projection** refers to seeing our own unpleasant/unacceptable impulses in others. We "project" our undesirable traits onto others.
- **Displacement** describes focusing unpleasant emotions somewhere other than where they belong. Kicking the cat instead of yelling at your father is an example of "displaced" anger.
- According to Freud, **reaction formation** occurs when we repress an urge to behave in a painful or threatening way by doing the polar opposite of what we really want. Treating someone you strongly dislike in an excessively friendly manner is an example of reaction formation. Some suggest that those who feel homosexual desire may exhibit reaction formation by turning their homosexual urges into hatred for all homosexuals.
- **Sublimation** refers to channeling primitive sexual and aggressive impulses into socially acceptable activities. Instead of punching your mom when you are angry with her, you sublimate the impulse by going to the gym to punch a punching bag.
- **Regression** describes an unconscious effort to defend the ego from stress by reverting to behavior characteristic of a younger age. Adults who, when under extreme stress, behave childishly, are said to have "regressed."

Freud's daughter Anna described several other defense mechanisms including: compensation, dissociation, escapism, humor, idealization, intellectualization, introjection, inversion, minimizing, splitting, and substitution.

Freud explained personality development in terms of **psychosexual stages**. Freud strongly believed that all mental illnesses were rooted in a failure to move properly through the psychosexual stages. Freud named each stage for the body part that was thought to be the focus of sexual gratification during that stage.

Freud thought that during the **oral stage** (the first year of life), gratification was mouth-oriented. According to Freud, sucking and chewing gratified the libidinal impulses. Too much or too little oral gratification permanently damaged personality development. Freud believed that overeating smoking gum chewers had **oral personalities** and were **fixated** on making up for missed oral gratification during the first year of life.

Freud noted that during toilet training (around age two), parents and children were very interested in poopy. He called that stage the **anal stage**. During the anal stage gratification centers on feces, parental expectations, training, and discipline techniques. Freud described adults who did not move (no pun intended) properly through the anal stage as **anal-retentive** (overly fastidious and neat) or **anal-expulsive** (overly messy and disorganized).

Freud theorized that during the **phallic stage** (age 3 to 6) children gratified their libido's impulses through their genitals. During this stage children begin to learn sex-role identities, modesty, and attitudes about sexuality. Freud believed that during this stage boys have erotic feelings toward their mother (the **Oedipal conflict**) and girls toward their father (**Electra conflict**). Freud believed that **penis envy** (girls) and **castration anxiety** (boys) were "normal" universal feelings during this stage and part of every family's sexual **family drama**. Freud suggested that excessively vain and proud adults (**phallic character**), aggressive women (**castrating female**) and **homosexuality** stemmed from failure to resolve sexual conflicts in the family drama.

Freud believed that during the **latency stage** (age 6 to 12) sexual urges were dormant. During this stage, we are thought to repress sexual impulses by channeling the libido's energy into school, athletics, and same-sex friendships.

We spend the rest of our lives in the **genital stage,** beginning at puberty, repressing or redirecting sexual libidinal energy.

Theories of Personality: Carl Jung

The Swiss Reformed Church, in which Carl Jung's (pronounced Yoong) father was a clergyman, affirmed the Bible as the sole and infallible source of God's revelation and Mankind's sin nature (original sin). In the Jung household, young Carl probably learned that Jesus Christ was the only Savior and that salvation comes by faith in Christ. Jung's theory of personality and psychotherapy however, reflects a greater influence of his mentor, Dr. Sigmund Freud.

Sigmund Freud's atheism was clear. Freud saw God as a universal obsessional neurosis. To Freud, religion was pathologic. Carl Jung viewed religions as beneficial myths. Jung's belief in the benefit of religion make his ideas more acceptable to many in Christendom, but to Jung, Christ and Buddha, as myths, were equal. His denial of the objective truth of the Christian worldview and his use of occultic practices requires Christians to approach his theories with extra discernment.

Jung was closely associated with Freud personally and professionally. Although their relationship ended in disagreement over Freud's emphasis on the sexual nature of personality development (they were enemies at the end of their careers), Jung's theory is grounded in Freud (**Neo-Freudian**). Whereas Freud focused on sex, Jung emphasized the unconscious and barely mentioned sex.

Carl Jung called his personality theory **analytic psychology**. Jung believed that the **psyche** (mind) existed in three levels; the **conscious** (comparable to Freud's Ego), the **personal unconscious** (comparable to the Id), and the **collective unconscious**. Jung described the collective unconscious as a repository of the collective experiences of all Mankind. Jung suggested that the collective unconscious evolved and was passed genetically from generation to generation. Jung believed that the collective unconscious contained primitive stories and symbols passed down from our ancestors.

Jung believed that forgotten experiences collected in our personal unconscious. The emotional experience of those memories cluster in emotion-laden themes or associations (**complexes**) that affect our behavior.

Jung "received" insights into his theories from a "spirit" by the name of Philemon. Jung believed Philemon was more than the product of his own unconscious. Jung communicated with Philemon much like a channelor or medium might communicate with the spirit world.

Jung was particularly interested in dreams, particularly in the dream themes common to all cultures. Common dream themes led to Jung's description of archetypes. **Archetypes** are universal images and universal tendencies to experience things in a particular way. Archetypes are the filters through which we are thought to behave and interpret experiences. For example, the **persona** is a universal way of experiencing social situations. According to Jung, Mankind displays a persona (mask) in social situations. Persona is that part of our psyche that we allow others to see. The **shadow** is an archetypal image of that part of our psyche we do not want others to see. Jung identified several archetypes including death, anima (our feminine side), animus (our masculine side), birth, power, the hero, the child, the wise old man, the earth mother, the demon, the god, the snake, and the boogieman.

Jung described personality traits in terms of introversion, extroversion, thinking type, feeling type, sensation type, and intuitive type. His traits are the basis of the Myer's-Briggs Type Indicator and correlate well with three of the "Big Five" traits described earlier.

Theories of Personality: Alfred Adler

Strict behaviorists reject the concept of personality. Remember that strict behaviorism explains all behavior in terms of learning. Personality then is merely a pattern of learned behavior. Freud believed internal sexual and aggressive impulses drove personality development. Jung believed that the internal collective unconscious shaped personality. **Alfred Adler** believed that external forces produced **feelings of inferiority** that provided the impetus for personality development.

According to Adler, **compensating** for feelings of inferiority shapes our personality. Adler described several terms that became part of the common language. **Inferiority complex** describes paralyzing feelings of inferiority. **Sibling rivalry** describes a competition between siblings for parental approval. Adler was an early supporter of the importance of **birth order** on personality development.

Adler believed that personality was largely formed by about age 6 as a direct result of family situations. The child who is able to overcome feelings of inferiority by being nice, or by becoming whiney and complaining, tend to habitually use that **style of life**.

Theories of Personality: Albert Bandura

Albert Bandura believed that personality developed through an interaction of behavior and cognitive processes. In his **social learning theory**, Bandura noted that through observation and modeling, we learn personality traits. Whereas the psychoanalytic personality theories viewed Mankind as passive and unconscious recipients of experiences, cognitive theories emphasize active mental processes. Bandura believed that we consciously regulate our behavior and develop personality through a number of cognitive processes including self-observation, judgment, attention, memory, motivation, self-regulation, expectation, and self-concept in a reciprocal relationship with our environment.

Theories of Personality: Carl Rogers

The humanistic (**person-centered**) personality theory is as closely associated with the work of Carl Rogers as psychoanalytic theories are with Sigmund Freud. Humanistic personality theories suggest that **self-actualization** is the sole force driving personality development. According to humanistic theories, all people have an inborn drive (**organismic sensing**) to achieve self-actualization. Organismic sensing or organismic valuing is thought to be an inherent ability to make choices that bring us closer to full self-actualization. Rogers' belief that Mankind inherently seeks the good that is naturally inside us stands in sharp contrast to the Biblical description of man's depravity.

Abnormal Psychology

This is probably the section for which you have been waiting. Next to understanding why we behave the way we do, understanding why everyone else behaves the way they do is what makes psychology so popular. This is also probably the most difficult section. As this text explained earlier, no topic in psychology comes closer to the core of Mankind's existence and to the heart of the Gospel message of sin and redemption than abnormal psychology. As a result, no part of the study of psychology causes more controversy and conflict than the study of the causes and cures of mental suffering.

Because, unlike some parts of psychology, abnormal psychology is so close to the foundation of one's worldview, there is often little room for compromise and disagreements tend to get ugly. One's worldview assumptions determine how one defines, evaluates the causes of, and treats mental illness. Some deny the existence

> The Scriptures plainly speak of both organically based problems as well as those problems that stem from sinful attitudes and behavior; but where, in all of God's Word, is there so much as a trace of any third source of problems which might approximate the modern concept of "mental illness"? (Adams, 1970)

of mental illness. Some explain mental illness in terms of sinful attitudes and behavior, and some, as has been the case for centuries, explain mental illness in terms of demonic activity. Some explain mental illness in terms of chemical imbalances, genetic errors, and social influences.

The overarching goal for this text was to help prepare Christian homeschool students for college-level introductory psychology. It is not the purpose of this text to settle any arguments between Christians. It is not the purpose of this text to settle arguments between psychologists and other psychologists or between Christians and psychologists. The purpose of this text is to expose you to the issues so that when you are taught that "all mental illnesses are the result of chemical imbalances in the brain" or that "all mental illnesses are the result of sinful behavior and disunity with God," you will know that it just might not be that simple.

This text uses the term "mental illness" for lack of a better term. The term mental illness refers to a group of brain disorders (again, for lack of a better term) characterized by severe disturbances in thinking, feeling, acting, and relating. The author acknowledges that many sincere and thoughtful Christians do not believe mental "disorders" exist It is not the author's intent to endorse or deny a disease model of mental illness. This text addresses the theories of biological causes for mental illness fully aware that many claim there is no evidence of a biological explanation for mental illness.

This text addresses extra-biblical approaches to the treatment of mental illness fully aware that many believe that the Bible is sufficient for all problems of living. This text addresses medicine and psychotherapy as forms of treatment for mental illness when many think medicine places people in bondage and that psychotherapy is a false gospel.

The Surgeon General's report on mental illness suggests that 23% percent of the U.S. adult population (44 million people) have a diagnosable mental disorder. The burden of mental illness on health throughout the world is staggering. The World Health Organization estimates that mental illness ranks second worldwide in the burden of disease. Nearly two-thirds of all people with diagnosable mental disorders do not seek treatment. The author suggests that Christians have a duty to quit arguing and address the problem.

What is abnormal?

To study abnormal psychology requires us to define "abnormal." Abnormal means "not normal." So, what is normal? Normal and abnormal behavior can be defined from several perspectives. Many Christians believe that pain, difficulty, hardship, suffering, and persecution is normal. Modern society's perspective is that pain, difficulty, and hardship are abnormal and to be avoided at all costs. Some define abnormal as behaviors, emotional states, or patterns of thought and perceptions that vary significantly (statistically) from the general population. Some define abnormal as behavior outside of socially accepted standards. Some define abnormal subjectively ("if I believe that my feelings are abnormal, then they are"). Some define abnormal in terms of dysfunctions in biological processes (diseases). Some define abnormal in spiritual terms of disunity with God and a failure to live according to moral guidelines. Others suggest that normal and abnormal are no more than value judgments of human diversity and that to label another's behavior as "abnormal" is to exercise power inappropriately.

Biological explanations of abnormal (the disease model) are predominant in modern psychology. Spiritual explanations of abnormal are predominant in Christendom. Most

> Although the disease model admits that environmental and social factors contribute to mental illness, they are relegated to a secondary status.

introductory psychology texts suggest that brain scans, analysis of neurotransmitters, and genetic analysis provide objective evidence supporting a disease model of mental illness. However, as you will learn in the Research Methods chapter, association does not necessarily indicate causation. Though research indicates that depressed people have lower levels of serotonin (a neurotransmitter), it is not necessarily true that low levels of serotonin cause depression. It could be that depression causes low levels of serotonin. A strictly naturalistic worldview must explain mental illness ultimately in biological terms. It is plausible and consistent with a Christian worldview that low levels of serotonin is caused by depression, and that depression, in turn, is caused by disunity with God and sinful behavior.

A little history

Throughout much of history, mental illnesses were explained in religious terms, often in terms of demonic influence. The mentally ill were viewed as less than human and were locked away like animals. Ancient treatments for mental illness included cutting holes in the skull to let the evil spirits out and torturing the ill to "bring them to their senses." More "modern" treatments included exorcism, lobotomies, electroshock therapy, insulin shock therapy, ice-bath therapy, and fever therapy. Until relatively recently, the mentally ill lived in asylums where they were often shackled, sedated, and sterilized. Concern for the rights of people in mental institutions and advances in psychopharmacology led to a shift in public policy known as deinstitutionalization. **Deinstitutionalization** describes the release of the mentally ill from mental hospitals into society. Today people cannot be hospitalized against their will unless they are an obvious threat to themselves or others.

Deinstitutionalization led to unintended consequences. The mentally ill were released to communities that were not prepared to care for them. The result was a rise in the number of homeless mentally ill in the 1970s and 1980s. There was also an increase in the number of mentally ill people in jails and prisons. Today, jails and homeless shelters serve as de facto mental institutions.

> A report released in 1990 declared that the Los Angeles Country Jail, with an estimated 3,600 inmates who were seriously mental ill, qualified as the largest "de facto mental hospital" in the United States (New York Times, 1990).

Classifying Mental Illnesses

Setting aside questions about whether mental illnesses exist, what causes them, and how to treat them, we can turn attention to describing them.

> **The DSM is often referred to as the "bible of psychiatry."**

This text uses the guidelines from the Diagnostic and Statistical Manual of Mental Disorders 4th edition (DSM-IV) of the American Psychiatric Association. Right or wrong, the DSM-IV is used by practically every mental health professional in the world. The DSM-IV provides a common language to describe and categorize mental disorders. The DSM-IV

> **The Washington Post reported that half of the experts involved in drafting the DSM had financial ties to the pharmaceutical industry.**

defines mental disorders as "clinically significant behavioral or psychological syndromes or patterns that are associated with distress (painful symptoms), disability (functioning), or an increased risk of suffering, death, pain, disability, or loss of freedom." The DSM-IV contains descriptions of close to 300 mental disorders, each precisely defined with a checklist of symptoms. As you read the names and descriptions of many of the disorders, you may begin to understand why critics suggest that the DSM-IV pathologizes some normal behaviors.

The DSM-IV acknowledges that determining what is a disorder and what is not a disorder is similar to the difficulties determining what is normal and what is not. The DSM-IV makes no assumptions that each category of mental disorder is a discrete entity with absolute boundaries dividing it from other mental disorders or from no mental disorder.

The DSM-IV contains 17 groupings of diagnostic categories.

1) Disorders usually first diagnosed in infancy, childhood, or adolescence.
2) Delirium, dementia, and amnestic and other cognitive disorders.
3) Mental disorders due to a general medical condition
4) Substance-related disorders
5) Schizophrenia and other psychotic disorders
6) Mood disorders
7) Anxiety disorders
8) Somatoform disorders
9) Factitious disorders

10) Dissociative disorders
11) Sexual and Gender Identity disorders
12) Eating disorders
13) Sleep Disorders
14) Impulse-control disorders not elsewhere classified
15) Adjustment disorders
16) Personality disorders
17) Other Conditions that may be a focus of clinical attention

Disorders usually diagnosed in infancy, childhood, or adolescence

Disorders usually diagnosed in infancy, childhood, or adolescence (commonly known as **developmental disorders**) include mental retardation, learning disorders, motor skills disorders, communication disorders, pervasive developmental disorders, attention deficit disorders, feeding and eating disorders, tic disorders, and elimination disorders.

Developmental disabilities

Developmental disabilities interrupt or interfere with normal mental development. Developmental disabilities affect social and cognitive development (communication, learning, judgment, interpreting, and responding to social cues). Developmental disabilities broadly affect mental development or affect an isolated part of mental development. Because developmental disabilities are generally present at birth, they are not considered to be mental illnesses, but people with developmental disabilities may also have a mental illness.

Mental retardation refers to significantly low **general intellectual functioning** as measured by the **intelligence quotient (IQ)** scores. Individuals with IQ test scores under 70 have **mild mental retardation**. IQ Scores under 50 indicate **moderate mental retardation**. Scores under 35 indicate **severe mental retardation** and under 20 indicate **profound mental retardation**.

Down Syndrome is the most common form of mental retardation. It is caused by a common genetic problem that can be diagnosed while a baby

> **For more information about Down syndrome visit the National Down Syndrome Society at:** http://www.ndss.org

is still in the womb. Normally, the nucleus of each cell contains 23 pairs of chromosomes, half of which are inherited from each parent. Down syndrome occurs when some or all of a person's cells have an extra full or partial copy of chromosome 21.

Learning disorders

Learning disorders are diagnosed when learning problems significantly interfere with academic achievement, typically involving some distinct type of information processing or skill. Learning disorders may affect selective performance, meaning that children with learning disorders may do well in all but one area of learning.

Learning disorders are thought to be brain-based information processing problems. They may affect input (getting information into the brain), organization (understanding or manipulating information), memory (storing and retrieving information) or output (expressing the information). The categories of learning disorders are Reading Disorder, Mathematics Disorder, and Disorder of Written Expression. The most commonly diagnosed learning disorder is **dyslexia**.

> For more information about learning disorders visit LD Online at http://www.ldonline.org/

Motor Skills Disorders

Motor skills disorders are characterized by significant impairment in the normal development of motor coordination.

Pervasive Developmental Disorders

Pervasive developmental disorders (including autism and asperger's disorder) are characterized by severe and pervasive impairment in several aspects of development. Autism and asperger's syndrome are two commonly diagnosed pervasive developmental disorders.

Autism is characterized by significant impairment in social interaction, significant impairment in communication, and restricted and

For more information about autism and theories of the causes of autism visit that National Autism Association at http://www.nationalautismassociation.org/

stereotyped patterns of behavior, interests, and activities. Autism generally appears before the age of 3 and is thought to impact the brain's development in the areas of social interaction, communication, and cognitive functioning. Autism is diagnosed in boys four times more often than girls.

Autistic savant refers to individuals with autism who have extraordinary skills not exhibited by most persons.

For more information read *Autistic Savant* by Stephen M. Edelson, Ph.D. at

http://www.autism.org/savant.html

Asperger's disorder is characterized by severe and sustained impairment in social interaction and development of restricted and repetitive patterns of behavior, interests, and activities. Unlike autistic disorder, Asperger's disorder is not characterized by significant delays in language, cognition, or self-care skills.

Attention-Deficit and Disruptive Behavior Disorders

Attention-deficit/ hyperactivity disorder (ADHD) is the single most common problem that brings children to the attention of psychologists and psychiatrists. ADHD is characterized as a persistent pattern of inattention and/or hyperactivity-impulsivity that is more frequent and severe than is typically observed in individuals at a comparable level of development.

According to the CDC, 7.74% of children age 4-17 have been diagnosed with ADHD.

What is ADHD?

ADHD is a fictitious "diseases" invented to sell prescription drugs?
ADHD is a very complex, neuro-biochemical disorder?
ADHD is just bad parenting?
ADHD is a genetic disorder?
ADHD is the result of too much television?

Children with ADHD typically are inattentive, easily distracted, have difficulty concentrating, are impulsive, and are hyperactive. Stimulants (like Ritalin and Adderol) often have a paradoxical effect on children with ADHD. Paradoxical refers to the fact that for many children, a stimulant serves to "slow them down."

Conduct disorder describes repetitive and persistent patterns of behavior in which the basic rights of others or major age-appropriate societal norms or rules are violated (aggression to people and animals, destruction of property, deceitfulness or theft, or serious violations of rules).

Oppositional defiant disorder describes a pattern of negativistic, hostile, and defiant behavior (often loses temper, argues with adults, actively defies or reuses to comply with requests or rules, deliberately annoys people, blames others for own mistakes, irritable, angry, resentful, spiteful, or vindictive).

Feeding and Eating Disorders of Infancy or Early Childhood

The feeding and eating disorders describe persistent feeding and eating disturbances. **Pica** describes eating non-nutritive substances (often dirt). **Rumination disorder** describes regurgitating and re-chewing food. **Feeding Disorder of Infancy or Early Childhood (failure to thrive)** describes the persistent failure to eat adequately.

Tic Disorders

A tic is a sudden, rapid, recurrent, nonrhythmic, and stereotyped motor movement or vocalization. **Tourette's Disorder** describes a pattern of multiple motor tics and at least one vocal tic.

Other Disorders of Infancy, Childhood, or Adolescence

Separation Anxiety Disorder describes "inappropriate" or excessive anxiety concerning separation from home or from those to whom the child is attached (excessive distress in leaving, reluctance or refusal to go to school, fear of being alone, nightmares regarding separation, physical complaints when separation occurs).

Reactive Attachment Disorder (RAD) describes markedly disturbed and developmentally inappropriate social relatedness in most contexts before age 5. It is characterized by serious problems in emotional attachments to others. Some children with Reactive Attachment Disorder may also be overly or inappropriately social or familiar with strangers. The cause of Reactive Attachment Disorder is not known, but most children with RAD had severe problems or disruptions in their early relationships. Many were physically or emotionally abused or neglected. Many experienced inadequate care in institutional settings.

Delirium, dementia, amnestic, and other cognitive disorders

Cognitive disorders are abnormalities in thinking and memory that are associated with temporary or permanent brain dysfunction. The main symptoms of these disorders are problems in memory, orientation, language, information processing, and attention to task. Orientation describes awareness of your surroundings and circumstances.

Delirium describes a disturbance in consciousness that develops over a short period of time. Delirium is characterized by a reduction in clarity of awareness of the environment (memory impairment, disorientation to time or place, unable to name familiar objects, rambling or incoherent speech, illusions, delusions, hallucinations, or inattention). A key characteristic of delirium is its rapid onset (hours or days).

Dementia describes cognitive deficits that impair memory and cognitive functioning. Dementia is characterized by memory impairment, aphasia (a loss of the ability to produce and/or comprehend language), apraxia (loss of the ability to perform simple motor tasks), agnosia (inability to identify and name objects), an inability to think abstractly, or to plan, initiate, and sequence complex behavior. All dementias include memory loss. Dementias progress slowly.

Fifty to sixty percent of dementias are Alzheimer's type. **Alzheimer's disease** is named for Alois Alzheimer who first described it in 1906. Alzheimer's is a progressive and fatal brain disease that destroys

> **For more information about Alzheimer's disease visit the Alzheimer's Association at http://www.alz.org/**

neurons and seriously impairs cognitive abilities. Abnormal structures called plaques and tangles are thought to play a role in destroying neurons. **Plaques** contain deposits of protein that build up between nerve cells. **Tangles** are fibers of protein that form inside dying cells. Though most people develop some plaques and tangles as they age, those with Alzheimer's tend to develop far more. The plaques and tangles tend to form in a predictable pattern, beginning in areas important in learning and memory and then spreading to other regions.

Another common dementia is vascular dementia. **Vascular dementia** is caused by reduced blood flow to parts of the brain. Parkinson's disease, Huntington's disease, HIV, head trauma, Pick's disease, Creutzfeldt-Jakob disease, prolonged chronic substance abuse, and a host of medical conditions that are known to be associated with dementia.

Amnestic disorders (Amnesia) describe an impaired ability to learn new information or to recall previously learned information. Amnestic disorders are thought to be caused by head trauma, tumors, strokes, long-term chronic substance abuse, or environmental toxins.

Substance-related disorders

The DSM-IV classification of substance-related disorders includes about 120 disorders related to drugs of abuse, the side effects of medications, and exposure to toxins. It groups drug of abuse into 11 classes (alcohol, amphetamines or similar drugs, caffeine, cannabis, cocaine, hallucinogens, inhalants, nicotine, opiates, phencyclidine (PCP) or similar drugs, sedatives, and hypnotics). For drugs of abuse, the primary distinction is between substance abuse and substance dependence.

Substance abuse and substance dependence describe patterns of substance use. **Substance abuse** is characterized by recurrent drug use that results in failure to fulfill major obligations, use in hazardous situations (i.e. drinking and driving), legal problems, and continued use despite social or interpersonal problems.

> **Tolerance: A need for markedly increased amounts of the substance to achieve intoxication or the desired effect or a markedly diminished effect from same amount of the substance**
>
> **Withdrawal: The development of substance-specific symptoms due to the cessation of substance use that has been heavy and prolonged.**

Substance **dependence** is characterized by:

- Tolerance
- Withdrawal
- Using the drug in larger amounts or over a longer period than intended.
- A persistent desire or unsuccessful efforts to control use.
- Spending a great deal of time in activities necessary to obtain the substance.
- Giving up or reducing important activities because of drug use.
- Continuing to use the drug despite physical, psychological, or social/occupational problems.

Schizophrenia and Other Psychotic disorders

All the disorders in this section of the DSM-IV are characterized by psychotic symptoms. Though other disorders may include psychotic symptoms, psychosis is the defining characteristic of these disorders.

The word psychosis stems from the Greek psyche (soul/mind) and -osis (diseased or abnormal condition). In a general sense, psychosis is a "break from reality." **Psychosis** has come to be understood more generally as a severe disturbance in perception (hallucinations), thought (paranoia and delusions), speech, emotion, mood, orientation, organization, or serious dysfunction in daily functioning.

Hallucinations are perceptions of things that are not really there. They differ from illusions in that in an illusion an object actually exists but is misperceived or misinterpreted. The object or event being hallucinated does not exist. Hallucinations may be visual, auditory, tactile, olfactory, or gustatory.

A person experiencing **auditory hallucinations** "hears" sounds (humming, whistles, screams, clicking) or voices that are not really there. The person may hear one voice or many. The voices may be incomprehensible or understandable and may be perceived as the voice of someone the person knows (friends, family, or even "God"). The voices are often threatening and demeaning and may make commands or demands on the hearer. The person experiencing the voices may believe they originate from anywhere (the walls, the radio, or from heaven). Without treatment, the voices are often relentless.

Delusions are beliefs that are clearly false but that are believed to be true and persistently held. A person with a delusion is convinced that the belief is true and will hold firmly to the belief regardless of evidence to the contrary.

Some common delusions are:

- A belief that someone or something else is controlling thoughts or behavior ("the FBI is controlling my thoughts").
- A belief that others can "hear" thoughts.
- A belief that events, remarks, or objects in the person's environment have special and personal meaning ("the news anchorman sends me special information about how to save the world").
- An exaggerated belief in one's importance or a belief that one has special powers, talents, or abilities.
- A belief that he or she is being persecuted, followed, watched, cheated, drugged, spied on, or poisoned (the CIA put listening devices in my apartment).

Many people suffering from psychosis have disorganized speech. They may jump from idea to idea with little or no logical connection between ideas. They may get off-track (**derailing**), make up words, or link words together by sounds instead of meaning (**clang associations**). Many people suffering from psychosis have disorganized behavior. They may be child-like, silly, agitated, dress unusually, laugh at inappropriate times (**inappropriate affect**), or have an unusual gait, posture, or movements. They may lack emotional expression (**flat affect**), withdraw from activities, lack motivation, and fail to care for their basic hygiene (**negative symptoms**).

The DSM-IV describes several psychotic disorders, but the most common is schizophrenia. **Schizophrenia** describes a chronic, severe, and disabling condition that affects about 1% of the population worldwide and accounts for over 50% of the admissions to psychiatric hospitals in the United States. The set of symptoms known as schizophrenia are described in ancient literature, but the word "schizophrenia" is less than 100 years old. In modern psychology, the condition was first called **dementia praecox** (the dementia of youth) because the symptoms and behaviors generally appear in older teenagers and young adults.

The word "schizophrenia" comes from the Greek roots schizo (split) and phrene (mind) describing the fragmented thinking of people with the condition or their split from reality. Schizophrenia does not mean "split personality."

Schizophrenia describes the presences of delusions, hallucinations, disorganized speech, grossly disorganized or catatonic behavior, and negative symptoms. The DSM-IV describes five subtypes; undifferentiated type, disorganized type, catatonic type, residual type and paranoid type schizophrenia.

Paranoid type schizophrenia is the most common type of schizophrenia. It is characterized by prominent delusions that usually involve some form of threat or conspiracy.

The **disorganized type** is characterized by disorganized speech, disorganized behavior, and inappropriate or flat affect.

The **catatonic type** is characterized by disordered motor activity. Suffers may be immobile or wildly active with inappropriate or purposeless activity and postures.

The **residual type** is characterized by the absence of prominent **positive symptoms** (hallucinations, delusions, disorganized speech or behavior) but continued negative symptoms.

Mood disorders

The DSM-IV categorizes mood disorders as depressive and bipolar disorders. Within the two broad categories there are about 15 specific disorders. Depressive disorders, as the name suggests, are characterized by symptoms of depression. Bipolar disorders are characterized by symptoms of depression and mania.

> **Mood: An emotional state.**
>
> **Affect: The outward expression of a mood. A person with *flat affect* seems emotionless. A person with *inappropriate affect* may weep uncontrollably at something that seems harmless, or laugh hysterically at nothing in particular.**

Remember that the DSM defines mental disorders as "clinically significant" behaviors and symptoms that are disabling or bring a risk of suffering, death, pain, disability, or loss of freedom. "Major depressive episode" is the phrase the DSM uses to describe "clinically significant" depressed mood. Similarly, "manic episode" is the word the DSM uses to describe a "clinically significant" elevated mood.

A **major depressive episode** is characterized by a depressed mood most of the day nearly every day, decreased interest in activities, significant weight change, too much or too little sleep, fatigue, feelings of worthlessness or guilt, poor concentration or indecisiveness, and thoughts of death and suicide.

A **manic episode** is described as an abnormally and persistently elevated, expansive, or irritable mood. Manic episodes are characterized by inflated self esteem or grandiosity, decreased need for sleep, pressured, loud and rapid speech, flight of ideas, distractibility, increased goal-directed activities or psychomotor activity, and excessive involvement in pleasurable activities with a high potential for painful consequences (sky-diving, risky relationships). **Bipolar disorder** describes moods that alternate between major depressive episodes and manic episodes.

> **Grandiosity: An exaggerated sense of one's importance, power, or knowledge.**
>
> **Fight of ideas: A nearly continuous flow of disorganized thoughts, ideas, and speech.**

Anxiety disorders

It has been said that anxiety is a normal human reaction to stress. It has been said that anxiety is a sin. It has been said that anxiety is a normal human reaction to stress, but being constantly in a state of anxiety is a sin.

> **Assignment 12.3**
>
> **Read Matthew 6:25-34 and Philippians 4:6-7.**

The DSM does not address hamartiology (the study of sin). It does, however, provide a nomenclature for several varieties of disabling anxiety (panic).

Panic is the essential feature of most of the DSM's anxiety disorders. A **panic attack** describes the sudden onset of intense fear, apprehension, an urge to escape, and a sense of impending danger, doom, or death. Palpitations, sweating, trembling, shortness of breath, chest pain, nausea, dizziness, numbness, and chills accompany the feelings.

Anxiety disorders are linked to the context or triggers of the panic. **Generalized anxiety disorder** ("free floating" anxiety) is characterized by a generalized, nameless, and groundless feeling of anxiety. The feelings cannot be related to anything obvious in the physical and social environment. **Phobias** describe anxiety to specific objects or situations. A phobia is an irrational, persistent fear of or unreasonable desire to avoid certain situations, objects, activities, or people. **Agoraphobia** is characterized by anxiety and panic about being in places or situations in which escape would be difficult or embarrassing. **Social phobia** is characterized by a severe and persistent fear of social situations. The phobic fear might be of animals (spiders/snakes), the environment (heights/water), somatic (blood/dentists), or of situations (flying/elevators).

Obsessive-Compulsive Disorder (OCD) is an anxiety disorder characterized by recurrent, unwanted and intrusive thoughts (**obsessions**) and/or irrational urges to repeat certain behaviors (**compulsions**). Common features of OCD are checking (checking to make sure the front door is locked 10 times only to be anxious that the door is actually unlocked) and rituals (rigid adherence to a specific routine).

Posttraumatic Stress Disorder (PTSD) is linked to an extremely traumatic triggering event. Exposure to an extremely traumatic event that involved or could have caused death or serious injury, is thought to result in feelings of intense fear, helplessness, and horror, and in persistently re-experiencing the traumatic event.

Somatoform disorders

Somatoform disorders describe a category of disorders in which psychological problems take a physical form. Somatoform disorders are characterized by complaints of physical symptoms that are not explained by a medical condition.

Somatization disorder is characterized by many vague complaints with no known physical cause.

Conversion disorder is thought to be caused by acute stress. It is characterized by the loss of sensory (hearing/eyesight) or voluntary motor (partial of full paralysis) functioning. The loss of sensory or motor functioning suggests a neurological or general medical condition, but it cannot be explained by neurological or medical conditions.

Hypochondriasis (hypochondria) is an excessive fear of having a serious disease. Whereas people with somatization disorder have numerous physical complaints, hypochondriacs are likely to be obsessed with a specific illness.

Body dysmorphic disorder is characterized by an obsession with a defect in appearance. The defect may be entirely imagined or based on a very minor defect that other people barely notice.

Factitious disorders

Factitious disorder is characterized by physical or psychological symptoms that are intentionally produced in order to assume a "sick role." Factitious disorder differs from malingering. In factitious disorder the individual seeks to be a patient. Malingering is characterized by intentional symptoms faked for some gain (avoiding jury duty/collecting insurance money).

Dissociative disorders

Dissociative disorders describe a split or dis-association in consciousness, memory, identity, or perception. Feeling dream-like, unreal, or cut-off from the environment characterizes dissociative disorders.

Dissociative amnesia is characterized by temporarily forgetting personal information; usually because of a trauma.

Dissociative fugue is characterized by a temporary lapse of consciousness while performing a complex behavior.

The most dramatic dissociative disorder is dissociative identity disorder (DID). Formerly known as multiple personality disorder, DID is said to be the existence of two or more distinct identities or personality states that recurrently take control of an individual's behavior.

Sexual and Gender Identity disorders

The DSM-IV categorizes sexual dysfunctions, paraphilias, and gender identity disorders. **Sexual dysfunctions** are characterized by a disturbance of sexual desire or disturbance in the sexual response cycle. **Paraphilias** are characterized by sexual urges, fantasies, or behaviors that involve unusual objects, activities, or situations. **Gender identity disorders** are characterized by strong and persistent cross-gender identification.

> The American Psychiatric Association removed homosexuality from it listing of disorders in 1973. Many call for the APA to remove Gender Identity Disorder in the next edition.

Eating disorders

Eating disorders describe severe disturbances in eating. **Anorexia Nervosa** is characterized by a refusal to maintain a minimally normal body weight, intense fear of gaining weight, and a disturbance in the perception of body size or shape. **Bulimia Nervosa** is characterized by binge eating followed by inappropriate compensatory behavior (vomiting, laxatives, excessive exercising, fasting) to prevent weight gain.

Sleep disorders

Dyssomnias describe disorders of the amount, quality, or timing of sleep. These disorders include **insomnia** (not enough sleep), **hypersomnia** (too much sleep), **narcolepsy** (sleep when you least expect it), **sleep apnea** (sleep interrupted by breathing difficulties), and **circadian rhythm sleep disorder** (formerly known as sleep-wake schedule disorder).

Parasomnias describe abnormal behavioral or physiological events during sleep. The parasomnias include **nightmare disorder, sleep terror disorder**, and **sleepwalking disorder**.

Impulse-control disorders not elsewhere classified

Intermittent explosive disorder is characterized by episodes of failure to resist aggressive impulses leading to serious assaultive acts or destruction of property. The degree of aggressiveness is grossly out of proportion to any provocation.

Kleptomania is characterized by a recurrent failure to resist impulses to steal objects that are not needed for personal use or for their monetary value.

Pyromania is characterized by deliberate and purposeful fire setting.

Pathological gambling is characterized by persistent and recurrent gambling, preoccupation with gambling, needing to gamble with increasing amounts of money, repeated failure to stop or reduce gambling, restlessness or irritability when not gambling, gambling to escape from problems or unpleasant moods, lying to conceal gambling, committing illegal acts to finance gambling, or jeopardizing relationships, job, educational or career opportunities by gambling.

Adjustment disorders

Adjustment disorders describe the development of emotional or behavioral symptoms in response to an identifiable stressor (or stressors) occurring within 3 months of the onset of the stressor. The clinical significance is indicated by the distress or dysfunction that is in excess of what would be expected given the nature of the stressor. Depressed mood, anxiety, or both characterize adjustment disorders.

Personality disorders

Personality disorders describe enduring, pervasive, and inflexible patterns of thinking, feeling, and behaving that deviate markedly from the expectations of the culture. Personality disorders are characterized

> The term "personality disorder" replaced the word "neurotic" in the DSM-III.

by disturbances in cognition (ways of perceiving and interpreting one's self, others, and events), affect (the range, intensity, variability, and appropriateness of emotional responses), interpersonal functioning, and impulse control. Personality disorders are inflexible and maladaptive exaggerations of normal personality traits. The DSM-IV describes eleven personality disorders.

The **paranoid personality disorder** is characterized by a pattern of suspicion and distrust. Unlike paranoid schizophrenia, people with paranoid personality disorders are not delusional. They do not hear voices.

Voluntary detachment from social relationships and a restricted range of emotional expression characterize the **schizoid personality disorder.**

The **schizotypal personality disorder** is characterized by acute discomfort in close relationships, cognitive or perceptual distortions, and eccentric behavior. People with this disorder often misinterpret casual incidents as having special and personal meaning and are often superstitious and preoccupied with paranormal phenomena.

Of the eleven personality disorders, perhaps the most noteworthy is the antisocial personality, sometimes referred to as **psychopath** or **sociopath. Antisocial personality disorder** is characterized by disregard for and violation of the rights of others. Deceit and manipulation are central features of this disorder and the person with this disorder is guiltless, lacks a sense of moral responsibility (conscience), and feels no remorse about hurting other people or violating social norms. People with this disorder often appear charming, intelligent, poised, and calm. Some suggest that antisocial personality disorder is practically synonymous with criminal behavior.

> **Assignment: 12.4**
>
> **In your own words compare the description of antisocial personality disorder to definitions of the word "evil" and suggest explanations for psychologists' efforts to find a biological or social explanation for the "disorder."**

Borderline personality disorder (BPD) is characterized by pervasive instability in interpersonal relationships, self-image, mood, and extreme impulsivity. People with this disorder have a pattern of unstable and intense relationships and a persistently unstable self-image.

Excessive emotionality and attention seeking characterize **histrionic personality disorder**. People with this disorder are uncomfortable or feel unappreciated when they are not the center of attention and are often inappropriately sexually seductive or provocative.

The **narcissistic personality disorder** is characterized by a grandiose self-image, exaggerated sense of self-worth, and lack of empathy for others. People with this disorder care mostly about them, believe they are special or superior, and may be preoccupied with dreams of fame, success, or power.

The **avoidant personality disorder** is characterized by social inhibition, feelings of inadequacy, and extreme sensitivity to negative comments. People with this disorder may be unwilling to get involved with people unless they are certain of being liked and view themselves as unappealing and inferior.

A persistent and excessive need to be taken care of characterizes the **dependent personality disorder**. People with this disorder may have trouble making simple decisions without advice and reassurance and may want others to take responsibility for most areas of their life.

The **obsessive-compulsive personality disorder** is characterized by a preoccupation with orderliness, perfectionism, and control at the expense of flexibility, openness, and efficiency. A person with this disorder may be excessively devoted to work to the exclusion of leisure activities and friendships and may be unable to discard worn-out or worthless objects.

Treatment

In Chapter 6, this text examined the causes and cures of mental illness from a worldview perspective. This section names and describes several "major" approaches to treating mental illness.

> A good seminary education rather than medical school or a degree in clinical psychology, is the most fitting background for a counselor (Adams, 1970).

It is important to restate here that worldviews guide theories of the causes of and treatments for mental illness. Without agreement about the cause of mental illness, agreement about treatment is not likely.

Mental illnesses (assuming there are such things) are the result of spiritual problems (sin), biological problems (hardware malfunctions), or social problems (trauma and life experiences). Or, mental illnesses are the result of some combination of the three. Treatment approaches will therefore focus on spiritual problems, hardware malfunctions, or social problems. Some assert that one explanation and treatment approach excludes all others. Others believe that combining approaches is right and proper. For example, those who believe that it is possible to minister God's grace through Biblical means (a spiritual approach to treatment) and to use techniques discovered by modern psychology (psychopharmacology/psychotherapy) practice what is known as the **"integration"** of psychology and Christian worldview.

Spiritual Treatment

Spiritual treatments, in a broad sense, are treatments that rely on spiritual or religious means to treat mental illness. In that broad sense, there are probably hundreds of "spiritual" treatments for mental illness. For example:

- In past life therapy, the clues to solving the problems in "this" life are found in "past" lives.

- In polarity therapy, the therapist is said to adjust the patient's energy field in order to improve the functioning of the mind and body.

- In therapeutic touch, therapists are said to smooth-out irregularities in the patient's "energy field," divert excess energy back into the environment, and channel some of the limitless energy of the universe to "jump start" the weakened energies of the patient.

- In Organic Process therapy patients are taught to how to return to their "unobstructed and unfractured organic self."

These "spiritual" approaches seem clearly inconsistent with a Christian worldview.

A Christian understanding of spiritual "treatment" refers to the work of the Gospel message for salvation and the work of the Holy Spirit and the life of Christ for sanctification. Biblical Counseling (also known as Pastoral Counseling, Nouthetic Counseling, Care of Souls, and Spiritual Direction) views all mental illness as the result of sin and wrong patterns of thinking and behaving. A key characteristic of these approaches is the belief that all mental illnesses are, at their core, spiritual problems (sinful behaviors and wrong thinking). These approaches see the Bible as completely sufficient for dealing with all problems of living, including those described as mental illnesses. Sin is the only explanation for mental illness and the Gospel message of salvation and the Holy Spirit's work of sanctification is the only solution for sin. Biblical counselors present the Gospel, lovingly confront sin, and teach Biblical principles in order

> **All Scripture is given by inspiration of God, and is profitable for doctrine, for reproof, for correction, for instruction in righteousness, that the man of God may be complete, thoroughly equipped for every good work (2 Timothy 3:16-17).**

to produce maturity and Godly living in the life of the counselee. Many Biblical counselors believe that to use any technique, model, approach, theory, or method from modern psychology (not found in Scripture) is compromise (at best) or heresy (at worst). Critics of a spiritual approach suggest that it ignores social and biological components of mental illness and/or that it fails to avail itself of effective techniques from modern psychology.

> **For more information visit the International Association of Biblical Counselors - Counseling God's Way at http://www.iabc.net/counseling.html**

Biological treatment (Medication)

As noted earlier, the dominant explanations for mental illnesses today are biological. If one believes that the cause of mental illness is biological (chemical imbalances), it is logical that one would expect the solution to be biological. Many researchers believe that some form of chemical imbalance is involved in all thought, mood, anxiety, and behavior disorders. While a direct causal link between chemical imbalances and mental disorders has not been found, researchers have noted neurotransmitter-level differences between individuals who experience symptoms and those who do not. They suggest that low levels of neurotransmitters, high levels of neurotoxins, or low levels of some key vitamins, minerals, and amino acids play a role.

A "pharmacological revolution" began in 1952 with the discovery of the anti-psychotic drug chlorpromazine (Thorazine). Some compare the development of anti-psychotic drugs for mental illnesses to the discovery of antibiotics for infectious diseases, anticonvulsants for epilepsy, and anti-hypertensive drugs for cardiovascular disease. **Thorazine** and related major tranquilizers had a calming effect, alleviated hallucinations and delusions, and allowed many patients to live outside of mental institutions. By 1964, some 50 million people around the world had taken the drug. Thorazine played a major role in the de-institutionalization of the mentally ill during the 1960s and 1970s. Following Thorazine's success, many new drugs were developed to treat mental illnesses. In 1954, meprobamate (Miltown) was approved as the first **anxiolytic** (anxiety reducer) and in 1957 iproniazide was approved as an **anti-depressant**. In 1970, the FDA approved the use of lithium to reduce manic symptoms in bipolar disorder (**mood stabilizer**).

Psychoactive drugs alter the way neurotransmitters work. Certain neurotransmitters are associated with particular mental functions and mental illnesses. For example, too little serotonin is associated with depression and anxiety and too much dopamine has been associated with schizophrenia.

The drugs work by making more or less of a particular neurotransmitter available in the brain.

Psychiatric medications are typically classified according to the disorder for which they are most usually employed.

- **Antipsychotics** (Neuroleptics) are used to treat psychotic symptoms by blocking dopamine receptors.

- **Antidepressants** treat depression by increasing the availability of norepinephrine and/or serotonin at neural receptor sites.

- **Anxiolytics** are used to treat anxiety symptoms and sleep difficulties by enhancing the activity of the neurotransmitter GABA. GABA has an inhibitory effect on motor neurons, so enhancing its activity effectively slows nerve impulses throughout the body.

- **Mood stabilizers** (anticonvulsants) are medications that have **anti-mania** qualities and antidepressant effect and are often used in the treatment of bipolar disorder.

Critics of the biological (medication) approach to treatment suggest that the emphasis on psychiatric medications provides a false hope that a "magic pill" will "fix" all our problems and they suggest that the emphasis on alleviating symptoms with medications ignores underlying spiritual and social problems.

Therapy

Therapy (also known as psychotherapy, talk therapy, analysis, or counseling) is a general term that describes countless techniques by which therapists/counselors (usually trained professionals), enter into relationships with patients (clients/consumers) for the purpose of helping the patient with symptoms of mental illness, behavioral problems, or personal growth. Most therapies use only spoken conversation (hence the name; "talk-therapy"). Therapy can be provided on a one-to-one basis or in a group. It occurs face-to-face, over the telephone, or via the Internet. Therapy may be brief or extend, over months or years. Clinical psychologists, social workers, marriage-family therapists, expressive therapists, trained nurses, psychiatrists, psychoanalysts, mental health counselors, school counselors, and the clergy provide therapy.

Therapy is used to help people with symptoms of serious mental illness, to choose a career path, to solve relationship problems, or to deal with trauma, abuse, neglect, grief, disappointment, anger, and stress. Therapy can help repair self-concept, ease fears and anxiety, resolve conflict, improve communication, or to seek "the meaning of life."

Psychoanalytic or **psychodynamic** therapies look to the unconscious to discover and treat emotional problems (reduce anxiety and guilt). The therapist helps the client bring unconscious motivations and conflicts to light, to confront beliefs and actions, and to examine memories, events and feeling from the past for clues to current problems. Psychoanalytic therapies typically take several years.

Freudian Psychoanalysis seeks to recreate one's personality (thereby curing mental illness) by bringing past experiences to conscious awareness. By dealing with the issues that interrupted progress through the psychosexual stages to conscious awareness, Freud believed the ego was strengthened and better able to manage libidinal impulses.

Behavior therapy (also called behavior modification) refers to the systematic application of behavioral techniques to the treatment of behavioral disorders. Behavior therapy establishes rewards, reinforcements, and desensitization to change unwanted behavior. Behavior therapy focuses on current behavior and does not address underlying or unconscious issues or conflicts. **Exposure therapy** is a form of behavior therapy in which one is deliberately exposed to disturbing situations in order to learn to cope with them effectively. **Progressive desensitization** is a form of behavior therapy for people with fears of specific objects or situations. In progressive desensitization, the patient is taught relaxation techniques and gradually exposed to the source of fear over time.

Cognitive therapy seeks to correct **distorted thinking** (cognitive) patterns that lead to unwanted feelings and behaviors. Cognitive therapy presumes that irrational beliefs underlie behavioral problems. The therapist helps the patient identify and change conscious and unconscious beliefs and expectations. Though Christians, like anyone else, may hold irrational beliefs, it is crucial that the identification of

---

Examples of distorted thinking

Emotional Reasoning: Using emotion alone to determine truth. "I feel ugly so I am ugly

Dichotomous (All or nothing) Thinking. Interpreting situations only in extremes without considering the possibility of alternate interpretations.

Catastrophizing (Magnification): Expecting and looking for the worst.

Filtering. Focusing on the negative, magnifying the negative, and ignoring or minimizing the positive.

Personalization: A tendency to believe that "its all about me" and take responsibility for a negative events even if there is no reason to do so.

Mind-reading: Assuming that we know what others are thinking, feeling, and why they behave the way they do.

"rational" and "irrational" be examined in terms of underlying worldview. Many cognitive therapists define "belief in God" as an irrational belief. Like behavior therapy, cognitive therapy focuses on current thinking and not on underlying or past issues.

Cognitive-behavioral therapy (CBT) combines a cognitive and behavioral approach to recognize and change distorted thought patterns and unwanted behaviors. It is based on the premise that the way we think about a situation and the way we behave in a situation are more important than the situation itself. CBT is the one of the most commonly used approaches to therapy and research suggests it is an effective approach to treating many emotional problems.

Family Therapy (Systemic therapy, family systems therapy, couple/marriage therapy) focuses on relationships between people. Where other therapies focus on individuals, family therapists look deal with interaction patterns within a "system." This approach emphasizes the importance of family relationships to emotional health. Emotional or behavior problems in individuals are the expression (symptom) of problems in the family. By adjusting interactions within the family, the family functions more effectively and the individual members experience symptom relief.

Movement/dance/art/music/play therapy: Use creative expression to help patients express emotions. Play therapy is used primarily with young children to allow them to vicariously express thoughts and emotions.

Humanistic Therapy (Person-centered therapy/existential therapy): Humanistic therapy seeks to help the "client" find answers to his/her own problems. The humanistic approach presumes that "the good" is within us and that we intuitively know best what choices to make. When circumstances do not align with our intuitive sense of self, we experience anxiety and depression. Through a non-directive relationship of unconditional positive regard, the client directs the healing process.

Integrating Psychology and a Christian worldview?

This is important! The introduction to this text claimed that psychology is one of the most controversial and divisive academic subjects among Christians today. Chapter 1 asserted that psychology departments often are home to the most anti-Christian intellectuals on college campuses. The stated purpose of this text was to begin to prepare Christian homeschoolers for the worldview challenges of modern psychology. A second purpose of this text is to help Christian homeschoolers evaluate

Christian criticisms of psychology. Toward those ends, it is important to understand the claims of the extremes. You must understand why some Christians hate psychology and why some psychologists hate Christians. With that understanding, one can evaluate the history of the relationship between psychology and a Christian worldview and discover if there is middle ground between the extremes.

Assignment 12.5
Review the material at:
http://www.psychoheresy-aware.org/mainpage.html
http://www.eunacom.net/Watters_Doctrine.htm

For further study, review the material at:
http://www.angelfire.com/psy/idolatry/index.html
http://members.tripod.com/jdlarsenmn/christian_psychology.htm
http://www.newswithviews.com/Ohara/debbie16.htm
http://www.outsidethecamp.org/xnpsych.htm

The problem of relating psychology to a Christian worldview is old and new. Throughout the history of the Church, Christians have struggled with the relationship of "Christ and culture." Throughout the history of the Church, Christians have suggested approaches to relating a Christian worldview and the culture. Those approaches by extension apply to relating a Christian worldview with psychology. This section outlines models for relating psychology and a Christian worldview.

The Church historically responded to culture and science in one of three ways:

- Total rejection and unending conflict.
- Parallel independence.
- Mutual interaction and influence.

Total rejection and unending conflict (anti-psychology). Applied to psychology, this approach views psychology and a Christian worldview in terms of fundamental and insurmountable divisions. This position requires that we reject psychology completely and/or recreate psychology from a Christian perspective. Many thoughtful Christians hold this position.

Parallel independence. This position sees the differences in psychology and a Christian worldview as irreconcilable, but it recognizes that psychologists and Christians can each make contributions on important issues from different perspectives. This approach recognizes the value of psychology but places that value at different epistemological levels. For example, this position recognizes psychology's contribution to our understanding of the nervous system but might reject its approach to explaining mental illness. This approach acknowledges the value of psychological data, but requires that the data be filtered through a Christian worldview. Many thoughtful Christians hold this position.

Mutual interaction and influence presumes that "all truth is God's Truth" and that God reveals truths through the Bible and through psychological research. This approach presumes that valid findings of psychology and valid interpretation of the Bible will not ultimately contradict, that psychological insights are not inherently anti-Christian, and that psychology can contribute to our understanding of Mankind and to solutions to our problems. This approach seeks to create a Christian psychology comprising the unified truths of both psychology and a Christian worldview. Many thoughtful Christians hold this position too.

Chapter

13

Research Methods

Earlier this text noted that modern psychology emphasized empiricism. We learned that for many psychologists, empirical data is the only acceptable way of knowing. A Christian worldview recognizes the value of Biblical and supernatural knowledge. That distinction however, does not mean that empirical research is without value. To the contrary, throughout history a Christian worldview recognized the value of putting ideas to the test. Research methods describe how ideas are put to empirical testing.

What is research?

We learned earlier that the goal of psychology is to observe and describe, suggest meaning (understand), predict, and improve. Research is a systematic approach to those goals. That systematic approach is known as the scientific method. The **scientific method** is a standardized way of making observations, gathering data, forming theories, testing predictions, and interpreting results. Research is not simply gathering information.

- Research begins with a question or problem and a clear goal.
- Research requires a specific plan.
- Research requires the collection and interpretation of data.
- Research builds on previous research and contributes to future research.

Psychological research, like research in other fields must be:

- **Replicable:** Replicable means that others can repeat the research and get the same results. When researchers report results, they also describe their procedures in detail to allow others to replicate the results.
- **Falsifiable:** A hypothesis must be stated in a way that makes it possible to find it false.

- **Precise**: Accuracy and precision are particularly important in psychological research. Precisely defining (**operationalizing**) terms is crucial. For example, research into "socialization" of homeschoolers must precisely "operationalize" what socialization means. Operational definitions state exactly how variables will be measured.
- **Parsimonious**: The principle of parsimony (thrifty) means that researchers should apply the simplest possible explanation to the observations.

> Occam's Razor: **"One should not increase, beyond what is necessary, the number of entities required to explain anything."**

Research begins with a **research question** or **theory**. For example, if I noticed that the homeschool children at church seem better educated than the public school children, I might ask "Is homeschooling an effective way to educate children?" Research questions begin broadly but through a review of research literature, we discover what others have learned and our question becomes more focused. The research question is refined and focused into a hypothesis. A **hypothesis** is a testable prediction of what will happen in some circumstance. For example, "homeschool children will perform better on standardized tests than children who were educated in public schools."

Research terms

All research seeks to determine the relationship between variables. **Variables** are any event, condition, or behavior than researchers can measure. Gender can be "measured" as male or female. Age, test scores, time, intelligence, experience, education, grades, skills, and attitudes can all be measured.

Research hypothesis suggest that one variable causes or is related to change or differences in another variable. Therefore, in the example above, method of education (homeschool/public school) and standardized test scores are the variables.

Research distinguishes between independent and dependent variables. The **independent variable** is what the researcher manipulates or varies. The independent variable is the suspected "cause" in cause-and-effect relationships. In our example, method of education is the independent variable. If we had a hypothesis that Biblical counseling was more effective than Prozac in treating depression, the treatment approach is the independent variable. The **dependent**

variable is what changes as a result of changes in the independent variable. Change in the dependent variable is the result or outcome. The dependent variable "depends" on the independent variable. The dependent variable shows the "effect" in cause-and-effect relationships. In our example, the standardized test score is the dependent variable.

Subjects are the individual participants involved in a study. The collection of subjects is the **research sample**. The sample is drawn from and representative of the **population**. In our example, each student in the study is a subject; the students selected for the study comprise the research sample. The sample of homeschool student/public school students comes from the entire population of homeschool and public school students. Researchers study a sample and **generalize** the results to the population.

Ideally, research participants and circumstances are identical in every way except for the variable being studied. In reality, extraneous variables may affect the results. An **extraneous variable** is any variable other than the independent variable that affects the dependent variable. For example, if the homeschool students in our example were college-bound and took test prep courses but the public school students did not, college plans and test prep course attendance are extraneous variables.

Research must use valid and reliable measurement instruments. In our example, the standardized test is the measurement instrument. **Validity** is the research term that describes the extent to which the measurement instrument measures what it is supposed to measure. The SAT test may be a valid test of scholastic aptitude, but it is not a valid measure of weight, height or personality. **Reliability** describes the extent to which a measurement instrument produces the same result when researchers administer it to the same group of people at different times. A bathroom scale that says you weigh 125lbs one day and 250lbs the next is not reliable.

Bias in research refers to any influence that distorts the research findings. Bias can subtly create error in the research design, measurement, sampling, procedure, or choice of problem studied. Types of bias include sampling bias, subject bias, and experimenter bias.

If, in an effort to prove that homeschool students perform better on standardized tests than public school students, the researcher selected homeschool students with high GPAs, the sample selection was biased. **Selection bias** occurs when extraneous differences between groups are present at the beginning of the experiment. To control for selection bias, researchers use randomly selected participants. **Random Assignment** means assigning or selecting subjects based on chance and not human decision.

In medical research, some subjects who believe they receive medication, but in fact do not, report that they experience the effect of the medication. The placebo effect is a measurable, observable, or felt improvement that is not attributable to the experimental treatment. In psychological research, the placebo effect describes the phenomenon in which believing that something is going to happen tends to make it happen. To control for the placebo effect, researchers create an experimental group and a control group. The **experimental group** receives the experimental treatment. The **control group** receives a fake (placebo) treatment. Both groups believe they are getting the real treatment allowing the researcher to determine if the effect of the treatment exceeds the placebo effect.

Subject bias refers to the impact of the subjects' beliefs and expectations on the research results. **Single-blind** research, in which the subjects do not know if they are receiving a placebo treatment or the real treatment, controls for subject bias.

> ### The Hawthorne Effect
>
> Between 1927 and 1932 researchers at the Western Electric Company's Hawthorne Plant tried to discover the relationship of working conditions to worker productivity. The researchers manipulated the lighting, humidity, work hours, break schedules, and a number of other factors. The researchers were surprised to discover that regardless of the changes, worker productivity improved. The researchers concluded that productivity increased because the workers were pleased to receive attention from the researchers who expressed an interest in them. The term Hawthorne effect describes a measurement effect in which performance improves as a result of the psychological stimulus of being singled out and made to feel important.

Similarly, the researcher's expectations can subtly and unintentionally influence research outcome (experimenter bias). **Experimenter bias** occurs when the researcher's expectations influence the research results. To control for experimenter bias, researchers create a double-blind procedure in which neither the experimenter nor the subject knows which subjects receive the treatment and which do not.

Research designs

Psychologists use many different methods. The methods generally take one of forms: Qualitative research and Quantitative research.

Qualitative research designs

Qualitative research is a generic term for a type of psychological research that is not experimental. Qualitative researchers observe phenomena in the context of the "real world" or natural circumstances and examine those phenomena in their full complexity (it is not reductive). Qualitative research provides rich, in-depth, comprehensive, and subjective information. Because of the subjective quality of qualitative research, it was once frowned-on by strict empirical psychologists, but in many ways qualitative research is better-suited for psychological research than quantitative research. Qualitative research represents a way of "knowing" more consistent with a Christian epistemology than strict empiricism. In qualitative research, researchers describe what they observe and look for correlations. Qualitative methods include case studies, ethnographies, and phenomenological studies.

In **correlational** research, researchers do not manipulate variables; they look for relationships (**correlations**) between variables. Correlation means things occurring together. **Quantitative research** looks for causation (one variable causes another). **Qualitative research** looks for correlation or patterns (one variable related to another). Correlations make it possible to use the value of one variable to predict the value of another.

A **correlation coefficient** measures the strength of the relationship between two variables. Correlation coefficients are always a number between −1 and +1. Correlation coefficients close to +1 or −1 indicate strong relationships between variables. A

> There is a correlation between income and education level. Knowing that high income is correlated with years of education allows us to predict one's education level based on income.

correlation coefficient of zero indicates no relationship between the variables. A positive coefficient means that as one variable increases, so does the other. There is a positive correlation between education level and income (go to college!). A negative correlation means that as one variable increases, the other decreases. There is a negative correlation between absences from school and grades (an increase in the number of absences from school is correlated to a decrease in grades).

In **case studies**, researchers study a single subject, program, or event in depth, using interviews, observation, and testing to provide a detailed analysis of the "case." In **ethnographic** research, the researcher examines an entire group in depth. In **phenomenological** research, researchers seek understanding of people's perception and understanding of a situation or event. Numerous phenomenological studies followed the terrorist attacks of September 11, 2001.

Quantitative research designs

The goal of quantitative (experimental) research is to carefully and systematically identify cause-and-effect relationships. In simple quantitative research a single independent variable is manipulated and a single dependent variable is measured. The ideal quantitative research begins with two groups that are equal in every way. Both groups are measured by some characteristic (variable). One group receives the experimental treatment (**experimental group**) and the other does not (**control group**). Both groups are measured again by the same characteristic. Results from the two groups are statistically analyzed to determine if the difference between the groups is statistically significant and attributable to the treatment. If the characteristic changes for the group that received the experimental treatment but not for the control group, we can conclude, all other things being equal, that the treatment caused the change. The challenge of quantitative research is in assuring that all other things are truly equal.

Psychologists statistically analyze data to organize, summarize, and interpret the data they collect. Statistical analyses describe the results. Statistical analyses provide evidence that the measures were valid and reliable. **Inferential statistics** provide evidence that the effect of the experimental treatment was not just due to random chance (**statistical significance**). A finding is usually considered statistically significant if the result could be expected to occurs by chance 5 or fewer times out of every 100 times a study is done.

Conclusion

The study of psychology is about more than personality theories, mental illnesses, psychiatric drugs, and counseling techniques. It is more than learning to analyze, manipulate, or control people. You do not need to surrender your worldview in order to study psychology nor do you need to compartmentalize your faith. To study psychology, you do not need to adopt anti-Christian assumptions about the nature of God, Mankind, knowledge, right and wrong, and psychopathology. You can learn about the wonders of the human brain and behavior while maintaining respect for the complete inspiration and authority of the Scriptures. Conversations and debates with classmates and professors about the Christian perspective on psychology represent evangelistic opportunities. Your study of psychology can prepare you to think Christianly about psychology's influence in academia, the culture, and society. Your studies in psychology can help reduce the Church's misunderstanding and fear of psychology and help the Church fulfill its duty to minister to the world's psychological needs.

Your study of psychology will help prepare you to confront the criticisms of Christianity you may face in an introductory psychology course and to recognize when philosophical assumptions are presented under the banner of "science."

In your study, you join others in physics, biology, history, the arts, sociology, theology, and many other fields seeking a deeper understanding of all of God's creation. Christ is Lord of all indeed.

REFERENCES

Adams, J. E. (1972). *Competent to Counsel.* Philadelphia: Presbyterian and Reformed Publishing Company.

Adams, J. E. (1972). *The Big Umbrella: And Other Essays on Christian Counseling.* Grand Rapids: Baker.

Adams, J. E. (1979). *A Theology of Christian Counseling.* Grand Rapids: Zondervan.

Aigner, T. G. and Balster, R. L. (1978). *Choice behavior in rhesus monkeys: cocaine versus food.* Science 201 (4355), 534

American Psychiatric Association: *Diagnostic and Statistical Manual of Mental Disorders,* Fourth Edition. Washington, DC, American Psychiatric Association, 1994.

Astin, A. 1993. *What matters in college?* San Francisco: Jossey-Bass.

Beck, R. (2006). Defensive verses Existential Religion: Is Religious Defensiveness Predictive of Worldview Defense. *Journal of Psychology and Theology, 34*(2), 143-153.

Beck, J. & Banks, J. (1997). Integration training in the seminary crucible. *Journal of Psychology and Theology, 25* (2), 183-185.

Beck, J. (2005). *The Integration of Psychology and Theology: An Enterprise out of Balance.* Retrieved March 23, 2005 at
http://www.facultylinc.com/discipline/aip.nsf/0/884b35b83ae8f1e187256a3e00635be8?OpenDocument

Beck, J. & Banks, J. (1992). Christian anti-psychology sentiment: Hints of an historical analogue. Journal of Psychology and Theology, (20), 3-10.

Beechick, R. (1998). *Dr. Beechick's Homeschool Answer Book.* Pollock Pines: Arrow Press.

Bobgan, M. & Bobgan, D. (1977). *The End of Christian Psychology.* Santa Barbara: EastGate Publishers.

Bobgan, M. & Bobgan, D. (1979). *The psychological way/The spiritual way.* Minneapolis: Bethany Fellowship.

Bobgan, M. & Bobgan, D. (1987). *Psychoheresy: The psychological seduction of Christianity.* Santa Barbara: Eastgate Publishers.

Bobgan, M. & Bobgan, D. (1989). *Prophets of Psychoheresy.* Santa Barbara: EastGate Publishers.

Borg, W. & Gall, M., et al. (1989). *Educational Research: An Introduction* (5th ed.). New York: Longman.

Boring, E. (1957). *A History of Experimental Psychology* (2nd ed.). New York: Appleton - Century - Crofts.

Bouma-Prediger, S. (1990). The task of integration: A modest proposal Journal of *Psychology and Theology*, 18, 21-31.

Bufford, R. (1977). God and behavior mod: Some thoughts concerning the relationships between Biblical principles and behavior modification. Journal of Psychology and Theology, 5, 13-22.

Carlson, C., Bacaseta, P, & Simanton, D. (1988). A controlled evaluation of devotional meditations and progressive relaxation. *Journal of Psychology & Theology, (16)*, 362-368.

Carlson, D. (1976). Jesus' Style of Relating: The Search for a Biblical View of Counseling. In Fleck, J. & Carter, J. (Eds.), (1981). *Psychology and Christianity: Integrative Readings.* Nashville: Abingdon.

Carpenter, D. (1998). Professional Outpatient Mental Health Service Delivery to the Church: An Analysis of Conservative Evangelical Attitudes in the Pacific Norwest (abstract). *Dissertation Abstracts International, (59)*12B.

Carter, J. D. (1975). Adams' Theory of Nouthetic Counseling. In Fleck, J. R., & Carter, J. D. (Eds.), (1981). Psychology *and Christianity: Integrative Readings.* Nashville: Abingdon.

Carter, J. D. & Mohline, R. J. (1976). The nature and scope of integration: A proposal. *Journal of Psychology and Theology, (4),* 3-14.

Carter, J. D. (1977). Secular and sacred models of psychology and religion. *Journal of Psychology and Theology, (5),* 197-208.

Carter, J. D., & Narramore, B. (1979). *The integration of psychology and theology.* Grand Rapids: Zondervan.

Clark, R. E. (1953). The Spheres of Revelation and Science. What Are Their Limitations in Relation to Each Other? [Electronic version]. *Journal of the American Scientific Affiliation, (5).* Retrieved January 19, 2005 from http://www.asa3.org/ASA/PSCF?1953?JASA6-53Clark.html

Clement, P. W. (1974). Behavior Modification of the Spirit. In Fleck, J. R., & Carter, J. D. (Eds.), (1981). *Psychology and Christianity: Integrative Readings.* Nashville: Abingdon.

Clinton, S. M. (1990). The foundational integration model. *Journal of Psychology and Theology, (18)*2, 115-122.

Clouse, B. (1997). Can two walk together, except they be agreed? Psychology and theology--A journey together or paths apart? *Journal of Psychology and Theology, (25),* 38-48.

Cohen, E. J. (1977). Holiness and Health: An Examination of the Relationship Between Christian Holiness and Mental Health. In Fleck, J. R., & Carter, J. D. (Eds.), (1981). *Psychology and Christianity: Integrative Readings.* Nashville: Abingdon.

Cohen, M. (2003). *A Brief Survey of the History of Biblical Psychology.* Retrieved February 3, 2005 at http://www.mattcohn.net/history.html

Cohen, R. J. & Swerdlik, M. E. (2002). *Psychological Testing and Assessment.* Columbus: McGraw Hill.

Collins, G. (1975). Popular Christian Psychologies: Some Reflections. In Fleck, J. R., & Carter, J. D. (Eds.), (1981). *Psychology and Christianity: Integrative Readings.* Nashville: Abingdon.

Collins, G. (1977). *The Rebuilding of Psychology.* Wheaton: Tyndale House.

Collins, G. (1981). *Psychology and theology: Prospects for integration.* Nashville: Abingdon Press.

Collins, G. (1993). *The Biblical Basis of Christian Counseling for People Helpers.* Colorado Springs: Navpress.

Collins, G. (2000). An Integration View. In Johnson, E. L., & Jones, S. L. (Eds.), (2000) *Psychology & Christianity: with contributions by Gary R. Collins, David G. Myers, David Powlison, Robert C. Roberts.* Downers Grover: InterVarsity.

Colson, C. & Pearcy, N. (1999). *How Now Shall We Live?* Wheaton: Tyndale.

Cosgrove, Mark P. (1995). The Fruit of Integration: Results in the Teaching of Psychology. *Journal of Psychology and Theology, (23),* 289-95.

Crabb, L. (1978). Biblical Counseling: A Basic View. In Fleck, J. R., & Carter, J. D. (Eds.), (1981). Psychology *and Christianity: Integrative Readings.* Nashville: Abingdon.

Crabb, L. (1981). Biblical authority and Christian psychology. *Journal of Psychology and Theology, (9),* 305-311.

Daily, M. (2006). *Natural Science: A Classical View.* Retrieved from http://www.hedgeschool.com/scienceclassical.html on October 20, 2006.

Dockery, D. S. (2000). *Integrating Faith and Learning in Higher Education.* An address to at the fall meeting of the Fellows of the Research Institute of the Ethics & Religious Liberty Commission of the Southern Baptist Convention on September 20, 2000. Retrieved from http://www.pfm.org/AM/Template.cfm?Section=BreakPoint1&template=/CM/HTMLDisplay.cfm&ContentID=4737 on March 27, 2005.

Dueck, A. (1989). On living in Athens: Models of Relating Psychology, Church and Culture. *Journal of Psychology and Christianity, (1*8)1, 5-18.

Dykstra, Michelle L., et al. (1995). Integrating Across the Psychology Curriculum: A Content Review Approach. *Journal of Psychology and Theology (23),* 277-88.

Eck, B. E. (1996). Integrating the integrators: An organizing framework for a multifaceted process of integration. *Journal of psychology and Christianity, (15)*, 101-115.

Edwards, C. & Noebel. D. (2002). *Thinking Like A Christian Textbook.* New York: Broadman & Holman.

Edwards, C. (2001). *Postmodernism.* Retrieved from http://www.summit.org/resource/essay/show_essay.php?essay_id=148 on February 14, 2005.

Ellens, J. (1981). Biblical authority and Christian psychology II. *Journal of Psychology and Christianity, (9)*, 318-325.

Evans, C. S. (1976). Christian perspectives on the sciences of man. Christian Scholar's Review, (6), 97-113.

Evans, C. S. (1989). The Concept of the Self as the Key to Integration. Journal of Psychology and Christianity, (3)*2*.

Farnsworth, K. E. (1982). The conduct of integration. *Journal of Psychology and Theology, (10)*, 308-319.

Farnsworth, K. E. (1985). *Whole-Hearted Integration: Harmonizing Psychology and Christianity Through Word and Deed.* Grand Rapids: Baker.

Finney, J. R., & Malony, H. N. (1985). Empirical studies of Christian prayer: A review of the literature. Journal of Psychology and Theology, (13), 104-115.

Fishbein, M. & Ajzen, I. (1975). *Belief, Attitude, Intention, and Behavior: An Introduction to Theory and Research.* Reading: Addison-Wesley.

Fleck, J. R. & Carter, J. D. (1981). *Psychology and Christianity: Integrative Readings.* Nashville: Abingdon.

Foster, J. D. & Bolsinger, S. A. (1990). Prominent themes in evangelical integration literature. *Journal of Psychology and Theology, (18)*1, 3-12.

Foster, J. D. & Ledbetter, M. F. (1987). Christian anti-psychology and the scientific method. *Journal of Psychology and Theology, (15),* 10-18.

Ganz, R. (1993). *PsychoBabble: The Failure of Modern Psychology and the Biblical Alternative.* Wheaton: Crossway.

Gorsuch, R. L. (1986). Psychology and religion, beliefs, and values [Electronic version]. Journal of Psychology and Christianity,(5), 39-44. Retrieved April 3, 2003, from http://www.fuller.edu/sop/integration/Publications/gorsuch.pdf

Gorsuch, R. L. (2002) Integrating Psychology and Spirituality? Westport: Praeger.

Grace, C. & Ecklund, K. (1995) The Perils and Promises of Teaching Integration in Introductory Psychology. *Journal of Psychology and Theology, (23),* 296-302.

Grace, C. & Poelstra, P. (1995). Excellence in pedagogy: some obstacles to integration for the Christian psychology professor. *Journal of Psychology and Theology, (23),* 237-243.

Ham, K. (1987). The Lie: Evolution. San Diego: Creation-Life Publishers.

Hill, P. C. (1989). Implications for integration from a new philosophy of psychology as science. Journal of Psychology and Christianity, (8), 61-74.

Hilts, P. J. (1990). *U.S. Returns to 1820's in Care Of Mentally Ill, Study Asserts.* The New York Times. Accessed online at http://query.nytimes.com/gst/fullpage.html?res=9C0CE1DB163CF931A2575AC0A966958260&sec=&spon=&pagewanted=print.

Hodges, B. H. (1976). Toward a model of psychological man and his science. Christian Scholar's Review, (6), 3-18.

Hunt, D. (1987) *Beyond Seduction: A return to biblical Christianity.* Eugene: Harvest.

Ingram, J. A. (1995). Contemporary issues and Christian models of integration: Into the modern/postmodern age. *Journal of Psychology and Theology, (23)*, 3-14.

Jeeves, M. A. (1976). *Psychology and Christianity: The View Both Ways.* Downers Grove: InterVarsity Press.

Johnson, E. L. (1987). Sin, weakness, and psychopathology. Journal of Psychology and Theology, (15), 218-226.

Johnson, E. L. (1993). The place for the Bible within psychological science. Journal of Psychology and Theology, (20), 146-355.

Johnson, E. L. (1997). Christ, the Lord of psychology. Journal of Psychology and Theology, (25), 11-27.

Johnson, E. L. & Jones, S. L. (2000). Finding one truth in four views. In Johnson, E. L. & Jones, S. L. (Eds.), (2000) *Psychology & Christianity: with contributions by Gary R. Collins, David G. Myers, David Powlison, Robert C. Roberts.* Downers Grover: InterVarsity.

Jones, S. L. (2006). Integration: Defending It, Describing It, Doing It. *Journal of Psychology and Theology, 34*(3), 252-259.

Jones, S. L., & Butman, R. E. (1991). *Modern Psychotherapies: A Comprehensive Christian Appraisal.* Downers Grove: InterVarsity Press.

Kotesky, R. L., & Price, P. J. Undergraduates Developing Their Own Systematic Integration of Psychology and Christianity. *Journal of Psychology and Theology, (23),* 266-70.

Koukl, G. (1994). Monkey Morality: Can evolution explain ethics? Retrieved from http://www.summit.org/resource/essay/show_essay.php?essay_id=68

Larzelere, R. E. (1980). The task ahead: Six levels of integration of Christianity and psychology. *Journal of Psychology and Theology, (8),* 3-11.

Leedy, P. D. & Ormrod, J. E. (2005). *Practical Research: Planning and Design.* Columbus: Pearson.

Lewis, C. S. (1952). Mere Christianity. New York: Macmillan.

LifeWay Research (2007). Reasons 18 to 22 Year Olds Drop Out of Church. Retrieved October 1, 2007 from Http://www.lifeway.com/lwc/article_main_page/0%2C1703%2CA%25253D165949%252526M%25253D200906%2C00.html?

Matzat, D. (1996). The Intrusion of Psychology into Christian Theology. *Issues, Etc. Journal, (1)*9.

McGreer, C. (1998). Worldview and Righteousness. Retrieved from http://www.ifca.org/voice/98May-Jun/MCGREER.htm on March 27, 2005.

Moreland, J. P. (1994). *Is Science a Help or Threat to Faith?* Retrieved from www.summit.org/resource/essay/show_essay.php?essay_id=156 on February 14, 2005.

Morris, H. M. (1988). The Heritage of the Recapitulation Theory [Electronic version]. *Impact, (183)*. Retrieved at http://www.icr.org/article/287/ on October 20, 2006.

Myers, D. G. (1991). Steering between the extremes: On being a Christian scholar within psychology. Christian Scholar's Review, (20), 376-383.

Myers, D. G. (1996). On professing psychological science and Christian faith. *Journal of Psychology and Christianity, 15,* 143-149.

Myers, D. G. (1996). On professing psychological science and Christian faith. Journal of Psychology and Christianity, (15), 143-149.

Myers, D. G. (2000). A Levels-of-Explanation View. In Johnson, E. L., & Jones, S. L. (Eds.), (2000) *Psychology & Christianity: with contributions by Gary R. Collins, David G. Myers, David Powlison, Robert C. Roberts.* Downers Grover: InterVarsity.

Narramore, B. (1985). The concept of responsibility in psychopathology and psychotherapy. *Journal of Psychology and Christianity, (13),* 91-96.

Narramore, B. (1992). Barriers to the Integration of Faith and Learning in Christian Graduate Training Programs in Psychology. *Journal of Psychology and Theology, (20),* 119-26.

Narramore, C. (1960). *The Psychology of Counseling.* Pasadena: Zondervan.

Narramore, S. B. (1973). Perspectives on the integration of psychology and theology. *Journal of Psychology and Theology, (1)*, 3-18.

Narramore, S. B. (1997). Psychology and Theology: Twenty-five years of theoretical integration. *Journal of Psychology and Christianity,(25)1*, 6-10.

Nelson, J. M. (2006). Missed Opportunities in Dialogue Between Psychology and Religion. *Journal of Psychology and Theology, 34*(3), 193-204.

Nelson, J. M. & Slife, B. D. (2006). Philosophical Issues in Psychology and Religion: An Introduction. *Journal of Psychology and Theology, 34*(3), 191-192.

Niebuhr, H. R. (1951) *Christ and culture.* New York: Harper and Row.

Parrott, L. & Steele L. (1995). Integrating Psychology and Theology at Undergraduate Colleges: A Developmental Perspective. *Journal of Psychology and Theology,(23)*, 261-65.

Passantino, B. & Passantino, G. *Psychology and the Church: Can Psychotherapy Be Integrated with Christianity?* [Electronic version]. Christian Research Institute. Retrieved from http://www.equip.org/free/DP220-3.htm on February 14, 2005.

Petty, J. C. (1984). Christian psychological apologetic. Journal of Psychology and Christianity, (3), 8-17.

Powlison, D. (2000). A Biblical Counseling Response. In Johnson, E. L., & Jones, S. L. (Eds.), (2000) *Psychology & Christianity: with contributions by Gary R. Collins, David G. Myers, David Powlison, Robert C. Roberts.* Downers Grover: InterVarsity.

Ratcliff, D. (1978). Using Behavioral Psychology to Encourage Personal Evangelism. *Journal of Psychology and Theology, (6)*3.

Reber, J. S. (2006). Secular Psychology: What's the Problem. *Journal of Psychology and Theology, 34*(3), 193-204.

Rice, T. S. (2007). The Effect of a Seminar on the Integration of Psychology and a Christian Worldview on the Attitudes of Christian Homeschoolers. Unpublished Doctoral Dissertation.

Richardson, F. C. (2006). Psychology and Religion: Hermeneutic Reflections. *Journal of Psychology and Theology, 34*(3), 232-245.

Roberts, R. C. (2000). A Christian Psychology Response. In Johnson, E. L., & Jones, S. L. (Eds.) (2000) *Psychology & Christianity: with contributions by Gary R. Collins, David G. Myers, David Powlison, Robert C. Roberts.* Downers Grover: InterVarsity.

Robinson, D. N. (1972). *Readings in the Origins and Principles of Psychology.* Encino, CA: Dickenson.

Rushdoony, R. J. (1978). The Mythology of Science. Nutley: The Craig Press.

Sanderson, W. A. (1978). Christian empiricism as an integrating perspective in psychology and theology. Christian Scholar's Review, (8), 32-41.

Schaeffer, F. A. (1976). *How Should We Then Live: The Rise and Decline of Western Thought and Culture.* Old Tappan: Revell.

Schaeffer, F. A. (1981). *A Christian Manifesto.* Westchester, IL: Crossway Books.

Serrano, N. (2000). *Why a Christian Psychology is a Community Psychology?* Wheaton College. Retrieved at www.wheaton.edu/psychology/CCPC/Documents/Serrano.pdf on February 2, 2005.

Sharf, R.S. (2004). *Theories of psychotherapy and counseling: Concepts and cases* (3d ed.). Pacific Grove, CA: Brooks/Cole—Thomson Learning.

Slife, B. D. & Whoolery, M. (2006). Are Psychology's Main Methods Biased Against the Worldview of Many Religious People? *Journal of Psychology and Theology, 34*(3), 217-231.

Tan, S. (2006). Theoretical Issues in the Relationship Between Psychology and Religion: Some Comments on Reber, Nelson, Slife and Whoolery, and Richardson. *Journal of Psychology and Theology, 34*(3), 260-265.

The American Heritage Dictionary of the English Language (4th ed.). (2000). Boston: Houghton Mifflin.

Thompson, B. (2004). A Christian's Response to Humanism [Electronic version]. *Apologetics Press*, Retrieved from http://www.apologeticspress.org/rr/reprints/Christians-Response-to-Humanism.pdf on March 20, 2005.

Van Leeuwen, M. S. (1976). The view from the lions' den: Integrating Psychology and Christianity in the secular university classroom. Christian Scholar's Review, (5), 364-376.

Van Leeuwen, M. S. (1988). Psychology's "Two Cultures": A Christian Analysis [Electronic Version]. Christian Scholar's Review. Retrieved from http://www.cccu.org/resourcecenter/rc_detail.asp?resID=988&parentCatID=158 on April 3, 2003.

Vande Kemp, H. (1982). The tension between psychology and theology: The etymological roots. Journal of Psychology and Theology, (10), 105-112.

Vande Kemp, H. (1986). Dangers of psychologism: The place of God in psychology. *Journal of Psychology and Christianity, (14)*, 97-109.

Vande Kemp, H. (1996) Psychology and Christian spirituality: Explorations of the inner world. *Journal of Psychology and Christianity, (15)*, 161-174.

Vande Kemp, H. (1998). Christian psychologies for the twenty-first century: Lessons from history. Journal of Psychology and Christianity, (17), 197-209.

Veith, G. E. (1998). Educational Victory: How Christians can reclaim the culture. *World Magazine, (13)*24.

Vitz, P. C. *Psychology as Religion: The Cult of Self-Worship.* Grand Rapids: Eerdmans, 1977.

Watters, W. (1987). Christianity & Mental Health [Electronic version]. *The Humanist,* November/December, 5-11. Retrieved from http://www.thehumanist.org/humanist-content.html on February 2, 2005.

Vendantam, S. (2006). *Experts Defining Mental Disorders Are Linked to Drug Firms.* The Washington Post. Accessed online at http://www.washingtonpost.com/wp-dyn/content/article/2006/04/19/AR2006041902560.html.

Westendorp, F. (1974). The Value of Freud's Illusion. In Fleck, J. & Carter, J. (Eds.), *Psychology and Christianity: Integrative Readings.* Nashville: Abingdon.

White, J. (1987). Putting the soul back in psychology. Downers Grove, IL: InterVarsity.

Wilson, D. (n. d.). In a Multitude of Counselors There are Big Bucks [Electronic version]. Credenda/Agenda, (4)7. *Retrieved from http://www.credenda.org/old/issues/cont4-7.htm on April 8, 2005.*